100 Great Tapas

100 Great Tapas
Pippa Cuthbert

Photographs by Gareth Sambidge

BARNES
&NOBLE

NEW YORK

This 2007 edition published by Barnes & Noble, Inc.
by arrangement with Cassell Illustrated.

ISBN-10: 0-7607-8364-0
ISBN-13: 978-0-7607-8364-1

Edited by Barbara Dixon
Design by Ashley Western
Photography by Gareth Sambidge
Prop Styling by Harriet Docker
Publishing Manager Anna Cheifetz

Printed and bound in China

10 9 8 7 6 5 4 3 2 1

Contents

Introduction – The Tapa Experience

It's a balmy evening and I drag myself away from the Spanish sunshine and wafting smell of orange blossom to enter the cool interior of a bodega or wine bar. Multi-colored tiles line the walls, barrels of wine and sherry are stacked in the corner and whole cured hams hang from the ceiling. But what is really drawing me in are the aromas of plate after plate of food being placed on the bar.

These small plates of food are "tapas" and are the best introduction to the Spanish way of life. And what I love so much about tapas is that they are just that—a way of life, not just a way of eating. Although they are thought to have originated in the Andalusian city of Seville, tapas have become a huge focus of every Spaniard's life. At the end of a working day, locals will head to bars for their evening ritual of eating, drinking, and chatting with friends—a ritual that since the 1980s has become popular all over the world. It is really a civilized way of drinking in which people move between bars, socializing and catching up on the day's news, watching soccer and relaxing. It is customary to stand up at the bar to sample the tapas with a small glass of beer, wine, or sherry. Tapas bars serve as de facto living rooms since entertaining at home, outside of the family, is uncommon in Spain. In the local tapas bar everyone mixes, regardless of social and economic status. This movable feast from one bar to another is known as the "Tapeo" and dinner is finally eaten sometime after 9:00pm or even later in the warmer months of summer.

There are many myths as to the origin of tapas and how this way of eating came to be such a part of the Spanish culture. Some believe it was enforced by the Spanish King Alfonso X, who insisted, in an attempt to keep stagecoach drivers sober, that all inns provided food when serving wine. It seems, however, that the most popular myth is that establishments would place a slice of cured ham, cheese, or bread over a glass of wine when it was served to prevent insects from falling in. Whatever the real story, tapas have become an iconic symbol of the Spanish culture.

The criteria for the success of a tapa dish is ultimately that it tastes good. True traditional Spanish food is based on raw, simple ingredients and has its roots firmly in home and country cooking. The style is robust and unpretentious and appearance is secondary. Ingredients are inexpensive, reflecting seasonality; and regional and traditional diversity is still evident. This simplistic yet indulgent way of eating little plates of food one after the other, just to tide you over to the next meal, has huge appeal to many people. The hardest part is to not let yourself eat too many. My recipes aim to encompass the real spirit of Spain while adding a contemporary dimension. Basically any dish can become a tapas as long as it is served in small portions and, consequently, any of my tapas recipes can become a main meal.

There are a number of ingredients and flavors that distinguish Spanish food. If you have ever driven through the Andalusian countryside where olive trees line the horizon in every direction, or smelt the strong aromas of orange blossom in Seville or Valencia you will know what I mean. In Catalonia rice fields provide the basis for the authentic dish Paella Valenciana and the regions of Galicia and Asturias are renowned for their quality fish and shellfish. And while sometimes forgotten, the central plains of Spain produce the well-known Manchego cheese as well as numerous other sheep's cheeses. It is important also to remember the Moorish influences and their presence on the Iberian Peninsula as far back as the 7th century. The Moors brought with them exotic ingredients such as saffron, almonds, and peppers, which are typical of Spanish cuisine today. Spain is a vast country that stretches north–south from France to Africa, and east–west from the Mediterranean to the Atlantic. What unites the Spanish is their inclination to eat well, drink wisely, and ultimately enjoy life.

Spain has not only made a mark in the international culinary world for the excitement and variety that tapas can bring to our dining repertoire, but the likes of restaurants such as El Bulli, near Barcelona, and Arzak, at San Sebastian, have raised standards to another level. Their experimental cuisine, in which the science of food makes people stop and think, is opening up new doors for tapas. You will find my recipes cover everything you would hope to find in a tapas book, while adding new ideas to broaden our minds. While nowhere near as wacky and experimental as the food found at El Bulli, it's a chance for tapas to evolve. Most can be made quickly and easily, many can be made in advance and served at room temperature, while others can be partly prepared and finished off at the last minute. Basically any dish can become a tapas, so be imaginative and let the "Tapeo" begin at home... Salud!

Olives, Dips & Breads

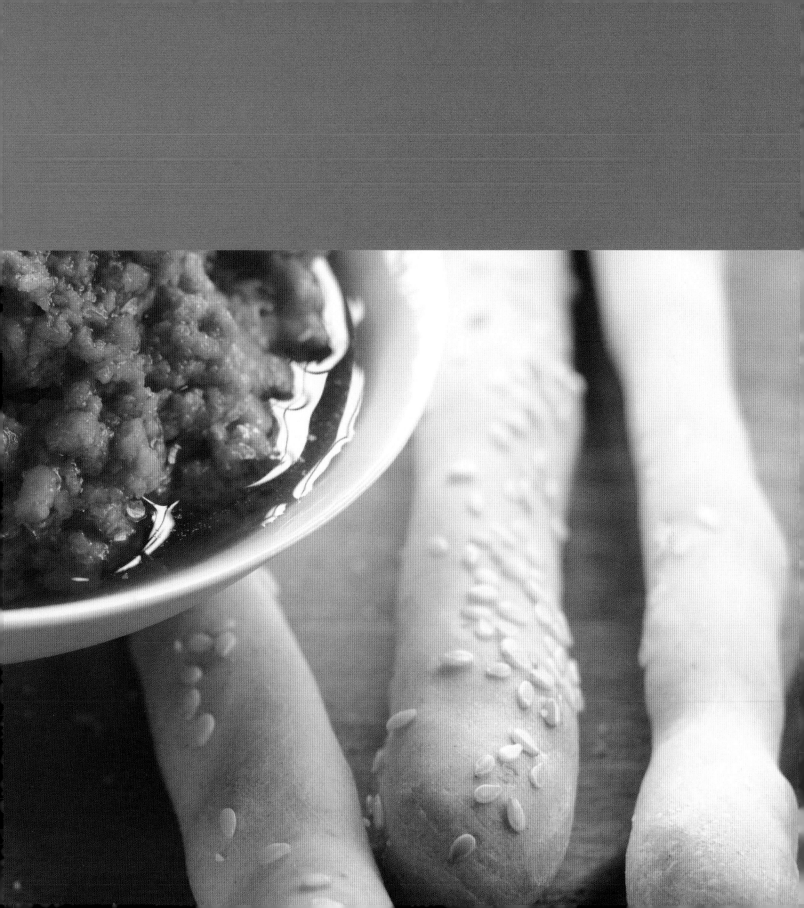

Andalusia is the land of olives. You may think it is sacrilege to fry olives
—I did at first and am still not sure I'm convinced! But sometimes,
when they are in such abundance, it makes a nice change.

Andalusian Fried Olives

⅞ cup/100 g all-purpose flour, for coating

1 egg, beaten

1 cup/100 g dried breadcrumbs

3 cups/500 g large stuffed green olives, of your choice

3–4 cups/ 750 ml–1 liter vegetable or sunflower oil

Serves 4–6 as part of a selection of tapas

Put the flour, egg, and breadcrumbs in three separate bowls and line them up in order. Coat the olives in the flour, dip them into the beaten egg, then coat in the breadcrumbs. Set aside on a plate while you heat the oil.

Put the vegetable or sunflower oil in a large, heavy-bottomed saucepan and heat to 375°F/190°C, or until a small cube of bread turns golden in about 30 seconds.

Fry the olives in the oil for 1–2 minutes, or until golden brown.

Using a slotted spoon, transfer to a plate and serve hot with a glass of chilled sherry.

Salted almonds are great as a tapa or just as a pre-dinner nibble with drinks. They can be made in advance and stored in a jar or airtight container until needed. Experiment with different flavors—chili or cayenne pepper works well, as does ground cumin or coriander.

For true authenticity, seek out Marcona almonds if you can. These famously round almonds are from the Valencia and Alicante regions of Spain and have a rich, buttery, sweet flavor and a creamy texture.

Lemon Salted Almonds

1 tablespoon butter

2¾ cups/300 g blanched almonds

1 tablespoon sea salt

1 tablespoon freshly ground black pepper

zest of 1 lemon

Makes 11 oz/300 g

Melt the butter in a large, nonstick skillet and add the almonds. Fry over a medium heat for 6–8 minutes, stirring continuously, until they are golden brown.

Turn off the heat and stir in the salt, black pepper, and lemon zest. Mix well, then arrange in a single layer on a large plate or tray lined with paper towels and leave to cool.

Store in an airtight jar until needed.

Salt and Fennel-Spiced Almonds

1 teaspoon fennel seeds

1 tablespoon sea salt flakes

½ teaspoon Spanish hot smoked paprika

1 tablespoon unsalted butter

2¾ cups/300 g blanched almonds (preferably Marcona)

1 tablespoon dry Madeira

Makes 11 oz/300 g

(Illustrated overleaf)

Heat a dry, heavy-bottomed saucepan or wok over a medium heat. Add the fennel seeds and salt and cook, stirring constantly, for about 3 minutes, or until the fennel seeds are lightly golden and aromatic. Transfer to a mortar and, using a pestle, grind to a fine powder. Stir in the paprika and set aside.

Melt the butter in the same pan and add the almonds. Fry over a medium heat for 6–8 minutes, stirring continuously, until they are golden brown.

Turn off the heat and stir in the Madeira, then add the fennel mixture. Mix well, then arrange in a single layer on a large plate or tray lined with paper towels and leave to cool.

Store in an airtight jar until needed.

Marinated olives are a deliciously simple tapa, which can be stored in the fridge for any unexpected guests. Using the basic formula below, try experimenting with different flavor combinations.

Marinated Olives

Each makes
11 oz/300 g

Fennel and Rosemary

3 cups/300 g green or black olives in brine, or a mixture

1 tablespoon white wine vinegar

3½ tablespoons extra virgin olive oil

1 garlic clove, peeled and sliced

1 tablespoon fennel seeds

3 sprigs fresh rosemary

Coriander and Lemon

3 cups/300 g green or black olives in brine, or a mixture

1 tablespoon white wine vinegar

3½ tablespoons extra virgin olive oil

1 tablespoon coriander seeds

zest of 1 lemon, cut into long shreds using a potato peeler

Chili and Thyme

3 cups/300 g green or black olives in brine, or a mixture

1 tablespoon white wine vinegar

3½ tablespoons extra virgin olive oil

½–1 teaspoon crushed dried chile flakes

3 sprigs fresh thyme

Drain the olives from the brine and rinse briefly under running cold water. Using a small knife, make a slit down the side of each olive right down to the pit.

Combine the vinegar, olive oil, and flavorings in a pitcher, then pour over the olives and mix well to coat.

Transfer the olives to an airtight container or jar and leave to marinate for at least 2 days for the flavor to develop, or for up to 3 months.

As well as being an addition to your cheese board, this recipe is great with broiled meats. I like to add it to a steak sandwich with plenty of garlic mayo or alioli, but to meet the tapas repertoire I've kept it small—simply spread on crostini with a slice of goat's cheese.

14 Caramelized Fennel and Onion Crostini with Goat's Cheese

1 tablespoon extra virgin olive oil

1 onion, peeled and thinly sliced

1 large fennel bulb, very thinly sliced

1 garlic clove, peeled and crushed

4 tablespoons superfine sugar

1 tablespoon wholegrain mustard

2 tablespoons white cider or sherry vinegar

Crostini (see page 23)

2 oz/50 g goat's cheese, thinly sliced

salt and freshly ground black pepper

Makes 24–30

Heat the olive oil over a medium heat in a nonstick saucepan and add the onion, fennel, and garlic. Stir until well coated in the oil and the onion and fennel start to soften but not brown. Increase the heat, add the sugar and stir constantly for a further 2–3 minutes, or until starting to brown.

Stir in the mustard and vinegar and season generously with salt and black pepper. When the liquid has evaporated, reduce the heat slightly and leave the mixture to caramelize and darken around the edges, stirring occasionally, for a further 8–12 minutes. Leave to cool.

Serve the fennel and onion mixture on prepared crostini and top with a slice of goat's cheese and a grind of black pepper.

Spread this over toasted breads, or use it to stuff cherry tomatoes. A spoonful can also be added to stews and casseroles as additional seasoning. It is an extremely versatile and delicious paste to keep a good stock of in the refrigerator.

This is a classic sauce from Catalonia, which traditionally contains romesco peppers and is often served with fish. In Tarragona, where it originates, it is made with both almonds and hazelnuts, but there are many versions today and mine is a slightly simplified one.

Black Olive Paste

Romesco Sauce

¾ cup/100 g pitted black olives

1 tablespoon capers, rinsed

6 canned anchovy fillets in oil, drained

small handful fresh flat-leaf parsley

2 tablespoons extra virgin olive oil

freshly ground black pepper

Makes about 5 oz/150 g

Put all the ingredients into the bowl of a food processor and whiz to a smooth paste.

Transfer to a bowl, cover with plastic wrap and refrigerate until ready to serve. This will keep for up to 1 month.

5½ tablespoons extra virgin olive oil

¾ cup/100 g blanched almonds

2 thick slices of white bread, crusts removed

2 roasted red bell peppers (see page 134), peeled and seeded

2 garlic cloves, peeled and finely chopped

¼–½ teaspoon dried chile flakes

2 teaspoons sherry vinegar or cider vinegar

salt and freshly ground black pepper

Makes about 8 fl oz/250 ml

(Illustrated overleaf)

Heat 2 tablespoons of the olive oil in a large, nonstick skillet. Add the almonds and cook, stirring, for 4–6 minutes, or until golden brown. Remove the nuts and drain on paper towels.

Put the bread in the pan and fry on both sides until golden. Remove from the pan and put in a food processor with the almonds, bell peppers, garlic, chile flakes, vinegar, and remaining oil. Blend to a paste and season to taste.

Chill in the refrigerator for up to 2 weeks.

It's hard to beat a plain bread stick with a cold beer.
They're satisfying to make and even more satisfying to eat.

Bread Sticks

1½ cups/350 ml warm water

¼ oz/7 g envelope dried yeast, or ½ oz/15 g fresh yeast

4 cups/500 g white bread flour, sifted, plus extra for dusting

1 teaspoon salt

2 teaspoons extra virgin olive oil, plus extra for greasing

2 teaspoon fine semolina

To flavor

choice of sea salt, sesame seeds, poppy seeds, rosemary, black pepper

Makes about 36

Pour ½ cup/100 ml of the warm water into a small bowl. Sprinkle on the yeast and leave for 5–10 minutes, then stir to dissolve.

Mix the flour and salt in a large bowl and make a well in the center. Pour in the olive oil and yeasted water. Using a wooden spoon, draw the flour in from the sides, adding the remaining water as needed to form a firm but sticky dough.

Turn the dough out on to a lightly floured work surface and knead until it is smooth and elastic—about 10 minutes. Cover the dough with a tea towel and leave to rest for about 10 minutes. Knead the dough for a further 10 minutes.

Preheat the oven to 400°F/200°C. Tear a small amount of dough (about 1 oz/25 g) from the ball at a time and, using the palm of your hand, roll to form a long, skinny, finger-like shape, about 10 inches/25 cm long. You can experiment with other shapes and sizes if you like, just adjust the cooking time accordingly.

Lightly oil a baking sheet and sprinkle over the semolina. Put the shaped bread sticks on the sheet and flavor with your chosen toppings. Bake in the oven for 15–20 minutes, or until golden and crispy. Transfer to a cooling rack and leave to cool. These can be stored in an airtight container for up to 1 month.

I'm always amazed at how good frozen broad beans are for this recipe, so don't worry if you can't get hold of fresh ones—at least it means you can make it year-round! Spanish or British broad beans are the best to use in this dish. Spend the time double shelling the beans once they are cooked—this gives a smooth, vibrant green spread. However, if you can't get hold of any broad beans, lima, or fava beans will make a good substitute.

Broad Bean and Roasted Garlic Spread

9 oz/250 g frozen or fresh broad beans, lima, or fava beans

2 roasted garlic cloves (see page 134), roughly chopped

a small handful of fresh flat-leaf parsley

juice of ½ lemon

¼ cup/60 ml extra virgin olive oil

salt and freshly ground black pepper

To serve

toasted sourdough bread, or Crostini (see page 23)

Manchego cheese

freshly ground black pepper

Makes about 9 oz/250 g

Bring a saucepan of water to a boil. Add the broad beans or lima beans and bring back to a boil, then reduce the heat and simmer for 2–3 minutes, or until tender. Drain the beans and rinse them under running cold water until cool enough to handle. Remove the outer shell from the broad beans and put the vibrant green centers into the bowl of a food processor (this is a labor of love).

Add the garlic, parsley, and lemon juice and whiz to combine. With the motor running, add the olive oil through the feed tube and continue blitzing to a smooth paste. Taste to season, then transfer to a bowl and refrigerate until ready to serve.

Serve on toasted sourdough or crostini with a few shavings of Manchego cheese on top and a good grind of black pepper. Keeps for 5–7 days.

Alioli is the Spanish version of aïoli, the rich, creamy, Italian garlic mayonnaise. Traditionally, in Catalonia it would include only garlic, oil, and salt. For a slightly more subtle and smoky flavor, try using a bulb of Roasted Garlic (see page 134) instead of six garlic cloves.

Alioli

6 garlic cloves, peeled and finely chopped

½ teaspoon fine salt

2 large egg yolks

¼ cup/60 ml light extra virgin olive oil

½ cup/125 ml vegetable oil, such as sunflower or canola oil

Makes about ½ pint/300 ml

Put the garlic and salt in a mortar and, using the pestle, grind to a paste. (Alternatively, use a large, heavy knife to mash and chop the garlic to a paste.) Put the garlic in a small food processor or blender, add the egg yolks and mix well. With the machine running, slowly add the combined oils through the feed tube, small quantities at a time, until the mixture is very thick. You may not need to use all the oil.

Use immediately, or transfer to an airtight container or jar and refrigerate for up to 2 days.

These cold cocktail stick snacks are served in bars throughout Spain. Be inventive and try spearing your own combinations on to cocktail sticks. This is just one idea to get you started but Ham, Melon, and Fig (see page 48) and Caramelized Onions Wrapped in Anchovies (see page 80) work on the same principle and are equally delicious. There's no end to the options!

Banderillas

12 cocktail sticks or wooden toothpicks

12 whole small gherkins, or 3 medium dill pickles, each cut into 4

12 pearl (silverskin) onions, or baby pickled onions

12 pitted green olives

2 red bell peppers, cut into 12 squares

6 guindilla peppers, halved

Makes 12

Skewer one of each pickle with the pepper pieces, onions and olives on a cocktail stick in any order. Try varying the order for esthetic appeal.

The anchovy topping is quite salty so make sure you spread the paste thinly on the bread. The parsley and oil help break through the saltiness—and so does a glass of sherry.

Anchovy Toasts

¼ cup/30 g finely grated Parmesan or Manchego cheese

1 garlic clove, peeled and crushed

a small handful of fresh flat-leaf parsley, finely chopped

1 oz/30 g canned anchovy fillets in oil, drained and finely chopped

1–2 tablespoons extra virgin olive oil

freshly ground black pepper

1 loaf sourdough bread (or other bread)

Serves 4–6 as part of a selection of tapas

Combine all the ingredients, except the bread, in a small bowl and, using a fork, mash together to form a rough paste. Add a little extra olive oil if the mixture feels too dry to spread.

Preheat the broiler to hot. Cut the bread into thin slices, about ¼ inch/ 5 mm thick. Using a knife, spread the paste over the bread slices in a thin layer until all the paste is used up or the desired number of toasts are made. (Any remaining mixture can be refrigerated for up to 3 days.)

Toast the bread under the broiler for 3–4 minutes, or until the topping is bubbling and lightly golden. Serve warm, sliced into triangles or into long strips.

Crostini are the basis of many tapas in Spain. They are usually kept simple with a slice of ham or a wedge of cheese, and you are often handed them when you order a drink at the bar. These can be made in advance and stored in an airtight container for emergency situations.

Crostini

1 large baguette, or thinly sliced sourdough bread

4 tablespoons extra virgin olive oil

Makes 24–30

Preheat the oven to 350°F/180°C. Using a bread knife, cut the baguette into 24–30 diagonal slices, about ½ inch/1 cm thick. Brush both sides of the bread with olive oil and place in a single layer on 1 or 2 baking sheets.

Bake in the oven for 10–12 minutes, turning once, or until golden and crisp. Remove from the oven and cool completely.

Serve topped with your topping of choice. These can be stored in an airtight container for up to 1 month.

These can be filled with anything you like. Try adding arugula and roasted vegetables or, for a nonvegetarian version, Serrano ham. Impressive, but simple to make, this is a great pantry recipe and a great party stand-by. Manchego is a Spanish sheep's cheese.

Quesadillas

4 small tortilla breads

2 tablespoons extra virgin olive oil

5 oz/150 g Manchego cheese, thinly sliced

2–3 roasted red bell peppers (see page 134), peeled and cut into strips

salt and freshly ground black pepper

Makes 12–16

Using a pastry brush, brush one side of each tortilla with olive oil. Place 2 tortillas, unoiled-side up, on a large chopping board or work surface. Place half the cheese and pepper strips in an even layer on each tortilla, then season generously with salt and black pepper. Place the remaining tortillas on top with the oiled side up.

Preheat a large, nonstick skillet until moderately hot. Cook the quesadillas one at a time. Carefully place the first one in the pan and cook for 2–3 minutes, or until the underside is golden and the cheese is starting to melt. Using a large palette knife, carefully flip the quesadilla over and cook for a further 2–3 minutes. Remove from the pan and cook the second quesadilla in the same way.

Cut each quesadilla into 6–8 wedges and serve warm.

This is great served as part of a platter with some thinly sliced toasted breads, pickles, Banderillas (see page 20), Caramelized Fennel and Onion Relish (see page 14) and a few crisp Belgian endive leaves. Make sure you buy fresh, plump and shiny-looking livers.

Chicken Liver Pâté

2¼ sticks/250 g butter, plus extra to seal

1 small onion, peeled and chopped

11 oz/300 g chicken livers, trimmed

3 bacon slices, chopped

1 sprig fresh thyme, leaves removed

scant ½ cup/ 100 ml fino (dry) sherry

salt and freshly ground black pepper

Serves 4–6 as part of a selection of tapas

Melt the butter in a large, nonstick skillet and sauté the onion for 2–3 minutes, or until cooked and translucent but not browned. Add the chicken livers, bacon, and thyme and sauté until the chicken livers are cooked but still slightly pink in the center and the bacon is browned—2–3 minutes.

Increase the heat and add the sherry so that it sizzles and the alcohol burns off. Remove from the heat and season generously.

Transfer the mixture to a food processor and whiz to a smooth paste. Pack the mixture into small ramekins or dishes and smooth off the surface, then place a thyme sprig and some coarsely ground black pepper in the center of each. Melt a little extra butter in a small saucepan and pour a thin layer evenly over the pâté. Allow to cool, then refrigerate until the butter has set. Use within 5 days.

The simplicity of this dish means that it must be made with only the best-quality tomatoes and extra virgin olive oil. Anything substandard will simply disappoint. In Andalusia, in the south of Spain, they make a version where the tomatoes are blanched, peeled, and blended to a smooth, frothy, and spoonable consistency that can be spread on to toasted bread as well.

Catalan Tomato Bread

1 small loaf crusty, country-style white bread (not ciabatta)

2 garlic cloves, peeled

about 4 very ripe vine-ripened tomatoes

extra virgin olive oil

sea salt

Makes 8 slices

Preheat the broiler. Slice the bread into 8 slices about ¾ inch/1.5 cm thick and lightly toast both sides. Rub the garlic over one side of each slice, then generously rub a tomato half over each slice so that lots of juice and seeds remain.

Transfer to a plate, drizzle with the olive oil, sprinkle with sea salt and serve.

An alternative to hummus that in my mind is even more delicious. When served with poached fish or fried sausages, it doubles up as an alternative to mash.

White Bean and Lemon Spread

400 g/14 oz cooked butter or cannellini beans, rinsed and well drained

2 garlic cloves, peeled and crushed

zest and juice of 1 large lemon

1 teaspoon fine salt

3½–5 tablespoons/ 50–75 ml extra virgin olive oil

1 small bunch of fresh flat-leaf parsley, chopped (optional)

freshly ground black pepper

To serve

Crostini (see page 23)

Roasted Cherry Tomatoes (see page 135)

Makes about 1 lb 2 oz/500 g

Put the beans, garlic, lemon zest, and juice, salt and black pepper in a food processor and whiz for about 30 seconds. With the machine running, pour in the olive oil through the feed tube until it forms a smooth paste. Stir in the parsley, if using.

Serve spread on crostini and topped with a roasted cherry tomato.

This sweet and smoky salsa is delicious served with meat, particularly as a dipping salsa for pork or beef skewers. For a more simple alternative, serve with Crostini (see page 23) or crusty bread.

Sweet Chile and Red Bell Pepper Salsa

2 roasted red bell peppers (see page 134), peeled and seeded

1 red onion, peeled and very finely diced

2–3 sweet red chiles, seeded and finely chopped

1 garlic clove, peeled and crushed

½ teaspoon Spanish sweet smoked paprika

scant ½ cup/100 ml extra virgin olive oil

juice of ½ lemon

a small handful of fresh flat-leaf parsley, roughly chopped

salt and freshly ground black pepper

Makes about 9 oz/250 g

Chop the roasted bell peppers into fine dice and put into a bowl. Add all the remaining ingredients and mix well to combine. Taste and season accordingly. Use within 5–7 days.

Why buy it when you can make your own? Okay, I know it's not always the right season, but when it is you can just make double and stock up for the year—it's much more satisfying and cost effective than store-bought.

Quince Paste (Membrillo)

4¼ lb/2 kg quinces, washed, cored and quartered

2 cups/500 ml water

juice of 1 lemon

superfine sugar

1 cinnamon stick

Makes 2½ lb/1.25 kg

Put the quinces in a saucepan with the water and lemon juice. Bring to a boil, then reduce the heat and simmer for 45–60 minutes, until they are soft.

Purée the fruit in a food processor, or push through a sieve. Weigh the puréed fruit and transfer the purée with an equal weight of sugar and the cinnamon stick to a clean, heavy-bottomed saucepan.

Cook the paste over a low heat, stirring, until the mixture thickens and you can hardly move the spoon through it—this will take about 1 hour. Keep stirring particularly when the mixture thickens so that it doesn't burn. The mixture will take on a pink color as it cooks. Be careful of it spattering.

Line a shallow baking pan with baking parchment and spread the mixture over it. Turn the oven to its lowest possible temperature and leave the mixture in there for 12 hours, or overnight. Alternatively, store in another warm place for 12 hours. The paste should be stored in an airtight container and will last for up to 12 months.

This light, buttery pastry is a great way to impress your guests. However, if time is limited, a great substitute is ready-made puff pastry from your local supermarket.

Empanada Pastry

4 cups/500 g
all-purpose flour,
plus extra for dusting

½ teaspoon fine salt

approximately
1 cup/250 ml water

2¼ sticks/250 g
butter, at room
temperature

Makes 1½ lb/750 g

Mix the flour with the salt in a large bowl and make a well in the center. Gradually mix in enough water to make a smooth, workable dough. Knead the dough for 8–10 minutes, then cover and chill for at least 30 minutes.

Roll the dough out on a large, lightly floured, flat surface, or floured board, into a rectangle about 17½ x 12 inches/45 x 30 cm and ¼ inch/ 5 mm thick. Spread the butter evenly over the dough and fold each short edge into the center, then the whole thing in half again, so that it is four layers thick. Cover and refrigerate for a further 30 minutes.

After 30 minutes, roll the dough out again to 17½ x 12 inches/ 45 x 30 cm and again fold into four, then return it to the fridge for a final 30 minutes. The dough is then ready to use.

Roll the dough out so that it is about ⅛ inch/2.5 mm thick and cut it into about 4 inch/10 cm circles for individual empanadas, or 2 large rounds for Galician-style empanadas. Return them to the fridge and work with only a few at a time. Fill and cook as directed in the recipe.

Meat & Chicken

These bite-sized, fried meatballs are found throughout Spain served with a variety of different sauces. These are albondigas caseras—meatballs served with a tomato, onion, and pepper sauce.

Spanish Meatballs (Albondigas)

9 oz/250 g (about 4) good-quality pork sausages

14 oz/400 g lean ground beef

¼–½ teaspoon dried chile flakes

1 garlic clove, peeled and crushed

1 small bunch fresh flat-leaf parsley, finely chopped, plus extra to serve

1 medium onion, peeled and very finely chopped

1–2 tablespoons all-purpose flour

2 tablespoons extra virgin olive oil

1 small red bell pepper, seeded and finely diced

½ teaspoon Spanish sweet smoked paprika

1½ lb/700 g passata (crushed tomatoes)

salt and freshly ground black pepper

Squeeze the sausage meat from its casings into a large mixing bowl. Add the ground beef, chile flakes, garlic, parsley, and half the chopped onion and mix thoroughly (it is easiest using your hands, but you can use a fork if you prefer). Season the mixture generously with salt and black pepper.

Sprinkle the flour over a chopping board and lightly flour your hands. Take heaped teaspoons of the mixture and shape into walnut-sized balls until all the mixture has been used.

Preheat the oven to 375°F/190°C. Heat 1 tablespoon of the olive oil in a large, nonstick skillet and fry the meatballs until brown all over. As they brown, transfer them to a large ovenproof dish that can hold them in a single layer.

Heat the remaining tablespoon of oil in the same skillet. Add the remaining onion, the diced pepper and paprika and sauté for about 2–3 minutes. Stir in the passata, bring to a boil and cook for a further 3 minutes. Season to taste.

Pour the sauce over the meatballs and cook, uncovered, in the oven for 30–35 minutes, or until lightly browned, turning once during cooking.

Serve the meatballs warm with cocktail sticks or wooden toothpicks.

Serves 4–6 as part of a selection of tapas

Thighs are the moist, dark meat of the chicken. It is sometimes a good idea to trim back the skin because it can be quite fatty. Thighs are also easily de-boned and can be stuffed and then secured with a couple of wooden toothpicks before being cooked in the same way as below. If stuffed, they will need a little longer cooking—do the skewer test to ensure they're cooked through.

Crispy Garlic Chicken Pieces

1 tablespoon extra virgin olive oil

2¼ lb/1 kg small chicken thighs, skin on

1 teaspoon Spanish hot smoked paprika

2 teaspoons dried oregano or thyme, or a mixture

3 large garlic cloves, peeled and crushed

Serves 6 as part of a selection of tapas

Preheat the oven to 400°F/200°C. Heat the olive oil in a large, nonstick skillet until hot. Add all the chicken pieces and the paprika and sauté for 4–5 minutes, or until starting to color.

Add the dried herbs and garlic and continue frying for a further 5–7 minutes, stirring regularly, or until the chicken is starting to turn crispy and is golden brown all over.

Transfer to a baking dish and cook in the oven for 15–20 minutes, or until the chicken is cooked and no pink juices run when a skewer is inserted into the thickest part of the flesh. Serve hot, warm, or cold.

These little bread towers are just one of the many combinations that can be secured together with a cocktail stick and served as a tapa. In Granada I was once served a piece of very thinly sliced roast pork on fresh white baguette—simple as that and absolutely delicious!

Marinated Pork and Membrillo Tapas

11–12 oz/300–350 g pork tenderloin, sliced into approximately 20 x ½ inch/1 cm thick rounds

1 small loaf sourdough or rye bread

5 oz/150 g Quince Paste (Membrillo, see page 30)

about 20 green olives stuffed with pimiento

For the marinade

2 tablespoons extra virgin olive oil

2 tablespoons fino (dry) sherry

1 teaspoon Spanish sweet smoked paprika

1 tablespoon fresh thyme leaves

1 garlic clove, peeled and crushed

juice of 1 small orange

Makes about 20

Combine all the marinade ingredients in a medium-sized bowl. Add the sliced pork and leave to marinate for at least 2 hours, or up to 24 hours.

While the pork is marinating, prepare the bread. Preheat the broiler. Slice the loaf into approximately 20 x ½ inch/1 cm thick slices and toast under the broiler on both sides until just golden. Cool, cut into finger food-sized pieces and set aside in an airtight container or bag until ready to serve.

Just before serving, heat a large, nonstick skillet to medium heat. Cook the pork slices for 1–2 minutes on each side, or until golden and cooked through.

Place one pork slice on each piece of bread, top with a cube of membrillo and an olive and secure with a cocktail stick or wooden toothpick. Serve within the hour if possible.

This is one of life's little indulgences. Juicy and succulent pork belly is not a tapa to eat every night if you're concerned about your heart. Pork belly has an equal proportion of fat and meat and this recipe is equally good cooked on the barbecue as it is in the oven.

Fennel and Rosemary Roasted Pork Belly

1 lb 2 oz/500 g pork belly (without rind), cut into 6–8 strips

2 sprigs fresh rosemary, finely chopped

2 garlic cloves, peeled and crushed

1 tablespoon fennel seeds

1 tablespoon extra virgin olive oil

2 teaspoons sea salt

Makes 12–24

Preheat the oven to 400°F/200°C. Place the pork in a single layer in a large roasting dish and set aside while you prepare the coating.

Combine the rosemary, garlic, fennel seeds, and olive oil in a small bowl. Using your hands, rub the mixture over the pork slices, then sprinkle generously with the salt.

Cook in the oven for about 30 minutes, turning once, until golden and crispy and the pork is cooked through.

Remove from the oven and cut each strip into 2–3 pieces. Serve warm with cocktail sticks or wooden toothpicks.

This is one of those tapas that comes into the category of a main meal downsized!

40 Mini Chorizo Sausages with White Bean Mash

7 oz/200 g cooked and drained white beans, such as butter or cannellini

1 garlic clove, peeled and crushed

3½ tablespoons extra virgin olive oil

12 (about 8 oz/225 g) mini cooking chorizo sausages

1 onion, peeled and very finely sliced

1 teaspoon superfine sugar

3½ tablespoons Rioja, or other red wine

salt and freshly ground black pepper

Serves 4–6 as part of a selection of tapas

Prepare the white bean mash first. Put the cooked beans in a food processor with the garlic and whiz several times. With the motor still running, pour the oil through the feed tube to form a slightly smooth mash. Taste and season accordingly, then put to one side.

Heat a large, nonstick skillet and cook the chorizo, turning frequently, over a medium-hot heat until the oils are released—about 4–5 minutes. Add the onion and sugar and sauté in the oil until the onion is soft and starting to caramelize. While hot, add the wine so that it sizzles and allows the alcohol to burn off. Stir for a further couple of minutes until it thickens, then remove from the heat.

When ready to serve, transfer the white bean mash to a heatproof bowl and microwave on High for 3 minutes, stirring once. Alternatively, heat 1 tablespoon of oil in a pan and sauté the mash until warmed through.

Place a small pile of white bean mash on each plate, top with two or three sausages and serve warm.

These little morsels are quite addictive, so be careful not to eat too many or you won't fit in any other tapas.

Chicken and Blue Cheese Croquettes

½ stick/50 g butter

¾ cup/75 g all-purpose flour

1¾ cups/400 ml milk

2 oz/50 g blue cheese, crumbled

1 tablespoon extra virgin olive oil

1 small onion, peeled and finely chopped

7 oz/200 g finely chopped chicken breast

1 tablespoon finely snipped fresh chives

1 egg, beaten

¾ cup/75 g dried breadcrumbs

vegetable or sunflower oil, for deep-frying

freshly ground black pepper

Makes 20

Melt the butter in a heavy-bottomed saucepan. Stir in the flour and cook, stirring, until it changes color slightly. Remove from the heat, add a little of the milk and, using a whisk, stir to combine. Slowly stir in the remaining milk until smooth, then return to the heat and continue stirring until the mixture becomes very thick. Stir in the cheese and set aside.

Heat the olive oil in a small, nonstick skillet and sauté the onion until cooked and translucent but not browned. Add the chicken and continue cooking for a further 5–7 minutes, or until the chicken is thoroughly cooked. Stir the chicken mixture into the cheese sauce along with the chives. Taste and season accordingly. Pour into a deep-sided baking pan and refrigerate for at least 2 hours.

Cut the mixture into 20 and shape into croquettes. Dip them, one at a time, in the beaten egg, then roll them in the breadcrumbs. They can be refrigerated at this stage until you are ready to cook them.

Heat the vegetable or sunflower oil in a heavy-bottomed saucepan to 375°F/190°C, or until a small cube of bread turns golden in about 30 seconds. Deep-fry the croquettes for 3–4 minutes, or until golden brown and hot through. Remove with a slotted spoon and drain on paper towels. Serve hot.

Croquettes require a very thick béchamel sauce, which is mixed with very finely chopped meat and left to chill. The mixture then becomes firm enough to shape into small sausage shapes or balls before being deep-fried and served hot.

Ham Croquettes

½ stick/50 g butter

¾ cup/75 g all-purpose flour

1¾ cups/400 ml milk

2 oz/50 g Cheddar or Manchego cheese, cut into small cubes

1 tablespoon extra virgin olive oil

1 small onion, peeled and finely chopped

3½ oz/100 g Serrano ham, finely chopped

1 egg, beaten

¾ cup/75 g dried breadcrumbs

vegetable or sunflower oil, for deep-frying

freshly ground black pepper

Makes 20

Melt the butter in a heavy-bottomed saucepan. Stir in the flour and cook, stirring, until it changes color slightly—this means the roux is cooked. Remove from the heat, add a little of the milk and, using a whisk, stir to combine. Slowly stir in the remaining milk until smooth, then return the pan to the heat and continue stirring until the mixture becomes very thick. Stir in the cheese and set aside.

Heat the olive oil in a small, nonstick skillet and sauté the onion for 2–3 minutes, or until cooked and translucent but not browned. Stir in the ham and remove from the heat. Stir the ham mixture into the white sauce, season with black pepper, then pour into a deep-sided baking pan and refrigerate for at least 2 hours.

Cut the mixture into 20 and shape into croquettes. Dip them, one at a time, in the beaten egg, then roll them in the breadcrumbs. They can be refrigerated at this stage until you are ready to cook them.

Heat the vegetable or sunflower oil in a heavy-bottomed saucepan to 375ºF/190ºC, or until a small cube of bread turns golden in about 30 seconds. Deep-fry the croquettes in batches for 3–4 minutes each batch, or until golden brown and hot through. Remove with a slotted spoon and drain on paper towels. Serve hot.

These have become a very popular party snack and work well as part
of a selection of tapas. I like them with something fresh and crisp
such as my Valencia Orange, Fennel, and Black Olive Salad (see page
124), but most of my friends seem to like them just the way they are.

Paprika-Glazed Pork Sausages

**2 tablespoons extra
virgin olive oil**

**2 tablespoons
honey**

**1 tablespoon
tomato paste**

**2 tablespoons
soy sauce**

**1–2 teaspoons
Spanish hot smoked
paprika, to taste**

**1 lb 2 oz/500 g
(24–30) cocktail
pork sausages**

**2 teaspoons
sesame seeds**

*Serves 4–6 as part of
a selection of tapas*

Preheat the oven to 350°F/180°C. Combine the olive oil, honey, tomato
paste, soy sauce, and paprika in a large bowl. Add the sausages and
mix to coat.

Put the sausages and most of the glaze into a baking pan or shallow
ovenproof dish and cook in the oven for 12–15 minutes, basting and
turning once or twice during cooking. Stir in the sesame seeds after
about 10 minutes. The sausages should be golden, sticky, and slightly
caramelized.

Serve warm with cocktail sticks or wooden toothpicks.

The use of intensely flavored and sticky pomegranate molasses adds a unique flavor to this dish and tenderizes the meat, giving a Moorish result.

Pomegranate and Yogurt-Marinated Lamb Skewers

4 tablespoons all-purpose unsweetened yogurt

1 tablespoon pomegranate molasses

1 teaspoon ground cumin

1 lb 2 oz/500 g lamb leg steaks, cut into 2.5–3 cm/1–1¼ inch cubes

1 pomegranate

a small handful of fresh flat-leaf parsley, chopped

freshly ground black pepper

12 small skewers (if wooden, soaked in water for 2–24 hours)

Makes 12

Combine the yogurt, molasses, and cumin in a bowl and season generously with black pepper. Pour the marinade over the lamb and stir until evenly and well coated. Cover and refrigerate for at least 1 hour, or up to 24 hours.

Just before you are ready to cook the skewers, preheat the oven to 400°F/200°C. Thread 3–4 lamb pieces on to each skewer and place on a large, foil-lined baking sheet.

Cook the skewers in the oven for 8–12 minutes, turning once or twice, or until golden and the lamb is cooked to your desired doneness.

Meanwhile, remove the seeds from the pomegranate and take off any white pith.

Serve the lamb warm sprinkled with pomegranate seeds and the chopped parsley.

These make a nice change from the usual asparagus wrapped in jamon or prosciutto. I love the way the leeks retain a little bit of crunch when you bite into them.

This is a selection of dried and cured meats. Choose amounts depending on how many people you are feeding. The following is a guide for 6–8 people.

Baby Leeks Wrapped in Jamon

12 baby leeks

6 slices (about 3 oz/ 75 g) of jamon or prosciutto

1 tablespoon extra virgin olive oil

sea salt and freshly ground black pepper

Makes 12

Preheat the oven to 350°F/180°C. Using a small knife, make a slit down the side of each leek just deep enough to remove the outer leaf. Trim both ends on an angle and wash the leek well to remove any dirt.

Wrap the central part of each leek in half a slice of jamon or prosciutto and place on a baking sheet. Drizzle over the olive oil and season generously with salt and black pepper.

Cook in the oven for 10–12 minutes, or until the leeks are soft and lightly browned. Serve warm.

Spanish Cold Cuts Platter

3–3½ oz/75–100 g thinly sliced Serrano ham

3–3½ oz/75–100 g thinly sliced cooked chorizo sausage

3–3½ oz/75–100 g thinly sliced lomo (pork loin)

caperberries

crusty bread or Crostini (see page 23)

extra virgin olive oil

Serves 6–8

Arrange the thinly sliced meats on a large platter and garnish with a few caperberries. Serve a plate of crusty or toasted breads on the side with some extra virgin olive oil for drizzling.

I remember sitting up at a bar in Granada at the end of a very long night. My friend Ian had dragged us around all the oldest and best bars in town and somehow there was still room for this little treat— you'll see why!

Complete simplicity but absolutely delicious, the saltiness of the ham offsets the juiciness and sweetness of the melon and fig.

Peas and Broad Beans with Pancetta

Ham, Melon, and Fig

1 heaping cup/150 g freshly shelled peas

150 g/5 oz freshly shelled broad beans, lima, or fava beans

2 tablespoons extra virgin olive oil

3 shallots, peeled and finely chopped

5 oz/150 g (about 1 heaping cup) pancetta cubes

1 large sprig fresh rosemary, finely chopped

salt and freshly ground black pepper

Serves 4–6 as part of a selection of tapas

Bring a large saucepan of water to a boil and cook the peas and beans for 3–4 minutes, or until just cooked. Drain then set aside.

Heat the olive oil in a large, nonstick skillet and sauté the shallots and pancetta until golden brown. Stir in the rosemary and sauté for a further minute.

Remove from the heat, stir in the peas and beans and season to taste with salt and black pepper. Serve warm.

12 cocktail sticks or wooden toothpicks

2 slices of Serrano ham, cut into 2 inch/5 cm slices

12 small cubes (about 3½ oz/100 g) honeydew melon

3 figs, each cut into quarters

Makes 12

Wrap one slice of ham around each cube of melon and skewer on to a cocktail stick. Skewer a piece of fig on each and serve.

Red peppers are generally juicier and sweeter that green peppers and so are often the preferred choice for roasting. Ramiro peppers are the long ones, sometimes called Hungarian peppers; however, regular sweet peppers can also be used in this recipe.

Ramiro Peppers Stuffed with Pork and Rosemary

3 large, red Ramiro peppers, 9–11 oz/250–300 g total weight

1 tablespoon extra virgin olive oil

1 medium onion, peeled and finely diced

1 garlic clove, peeled and crushed

2 sprigs fresh rosemary, finely chopped (about 1 tablespoon chopped)

¼ teaspoon dried chile flakes

450 g/1 lb ground pork

1 tablespoon tomato paste

5 tablespoons sweet Madeira

14 oz/400 g can chopped tomatoes

salt and freshly ground black pepper

Makes 6 tapas-sized portions

Cut the peppers in half lengthwise and place, cut-side up, on a baking sheet, then set aside.

Heat the olive oil in a large, nonstick skillet and sauté the onion for 2–3 minutes, or until translucent but not browned. Add the garlic, rosemary, and chile flakes and sauté for a further minute. Add the ground pork, increase the heat and cook until the meat is browned and cooked, breaking it up with a wooden fork or spoon as you go. When the meat has browned, lower the heat and stir in the tomato paste and then the Madeira. Cook until all the liquid has evaporated, then add the tomatoes and cook for a further 10 minutes. Season and set aside to cool slightly.

Preheat the oven to 375ºF/190ºC. Spoon the mixture into the pepper halves and bake in the oven for about 15 minutes, or until the peppers are cooked and the filling lightly golden on top. Serve warm or cool.

This is a chunky and hearty salad that can be served warm or cold. The juices from the sausages give the dish a golden glow and spicy note. Make sure you get the potatoes and chorizo golden and crispy and then the dish is easily eaten with cocktail sticks instead of a fork.

Crispy Chorizo and New Potatoes

1 lb 2 oz/500 g new potatoes, scrubbed

3 (about 11 oz/300 g) cooking chorizo sausages chopped into ½ inch/1 cm slices

2 sprigs fresh rosemary, leaves chopped finely

2 tablespoons dry Madeira

Serves 4–6 as part of a selection of tapas

Boil the potatoes for 8–10 minutes, or until cooked but still firm. Remove from the heat and cool them under running cold water, then cut them in half lengthwise on the diagonal and set aside.

Heat a large, nonstick skillet to hot and cook the chorizo for 2–3 minutes, or until the oils are released. Add the potatoes and rosemary and cook, stirring frequently, over high heat for a further 2–3 minutes, or until golden and crispy.

Reduce the heat and add the Madeira. Stir and leave to caramelize and brown for a further 2–3 minutes, stirring occasionally.

Serve warm with cocktail sticks or wooden toothpicks, or as a salad.

Chiles play an important role in Spanish cooking, adding to dishes not only heat but also distinct flavors. This tapa uses the chiles and seeds for heat and the paprika, a chile derivative, for flavor.

Peri Peri Chicken Nibbles

24 chicken wings

2–3 red chiles, stems removed, seeded and roughly chopped

4 tablespoons cider vinegar

4 tablespoons extra virgin olive oil

1 tablespoon cayenne pepper

2 garlic cloves, peeled and crushed

1 tablespoon Spanish hot smoked paprika

1 teaspoon fine salt

Makes 24 nibbles

Using poultry shears or sharp kitchen scissors, cut the tips from the chicken wings, through the joint. Put all the wings in a large plastic bag or nonmetallic bowl and set aside.

To prepare the marinade, put all the remaining ingredients in a food processor or blender and whiz to a smooth paste. Pour the marinade over the chicken and mix well until the chicken is evenly coated. Cover and refrigerate for at least 30 minutes, or up to 24 hours.

When you are ready to cook the chicken, preheat the oven to 425°F/220°C. Place the chicken in a roasting pan and cook in the oven for 15–20 minutes, or until cooked through and no pink juices are released when a skewer is inserted into the thickest part of the flesh.

Serve warm or cold with plenty of paper napkins.

In literal terms, empanadas are actually large pies and empanadillas are smaller pies. They can come with a range of fillings from pork to seafood and egg to vegetable. Spicy chicken is always a party pleaser!

Spicy Chicken Empanadas

1 quantity Empanada Pastry (see page 31), or 1 lb 2 oz/500 g bought puff pastry

1 tablespoon extra virgin olive oil

1 small onion, peeled and very finely chopped

1 garlic clove, peeled and crushed

1 teaspoon dried chile flakes

1 teaspoon ground cumin

½ teaspoon ground coriander

½ teaspoon ground cinnamon

11 oz/300 g (about 2 breasts) chicken breast meat, finely chopped

4 fl oz/125 ml passata (crushed tomatoes)

all-purpose flour, for dusting

¼ stick/30 g butter, melted

salt and freshly ground black pepper

Prepare the pastry and refrigerate until ready to assemble.

Heat the olive oil in a nonstick skillet and sauté the onion for about 2 minutes, or until translucent but not browned. Add the garlic, chile flakes, ground cumin, coriander, and cinnamon and sauté for a further minute. Add the chicken, increase the heat and cook until the meat is browned.

Lower the heat and stir in the passata, then cook for a further 3–4 minutes, or until the chicken is cooked and the mixture not too wet. Season to taste.

When you are ready to cook the empanadas, preheat the oven to 400°F/200°C. Roll the pastry out on a lightly floured surface to ⅛–¼ inch/3–5 mm thick and, using a 3½–4 inch/9–10 cm round cutter, cut out circles. Place a heaped teaspoon of the filling on one half of each round of pastry. Dip your finger in water and slightly dampen the pastry edges (to help them stick), then fold the pastry over the filling to make a half-moon shape. To seal the empanadas, pinch the edges of the pastry firmly together, then press down on the edges with the prongs of a fork to finish.

Brush the empanadas with melted butter and bake in the oven for 15–18 minutes, or until golden and puffed. Serve hot or warm.

Makes 24–30

Empanadas are traditionally deep-fried, but I prefer the slightly
healthier option of baking the parcels instead.

Pork Empanadas

1 quantity Empanada
Pastry (see page 31),
or 1 lb 2 oz/500 g
bought puff pastry

1 tablespoon extra
virgin olive oil

1 small onion, peeled
and finely diced

1 garlic clove,
peeled and crushed

1 sprig fresh
rosemary, finely
chopped (about
½ tablespoon
chopped)

¼ teaspoon dried
chile flakes

200 g/7 oz
ground pork

1 tablespoon
tomato paste

2 tablespoons
dry Madeira

all-purpose flour,
for dusting

¼ stick/30 g
butter, melted

salt and freshly
ground black pepper

Makes 30–36

Prepare the pastry and refrigerate until ready to assemble.

Heat the olive oil in a nonstick skillet and sauté the onion for about
2 minutes, or until translucent but not browned. Add the garlic,
rosemary and chile flakes and sauté for a further minute. Add the
ground pork, increase the heat and cook until the meat is browned and
cooked, breaking it up with a wooden fork or spoon as you go. When
the meat has browned, lower the heat and stir in the tomato paste,
then add the Madeira and season to taste. Cook until all the liquid has
evaporated, then take off the heat and leave to cool.

When you are ready to cook the empanadas, preheat the oven to
400°F/200°C. Roll the pastry out on a lightly floured surface to
⅛–¼ inch/3–5 mm thick and, using a 3½–4 inch/9–10 cm round
cutter, cut out circles.

Place a heaped teaspoon of the filling on one half of each round of
pastry. Dip your finger in water and slightly dampen the pastry edges
(to help them stick), then fold the pastry over the filling to make a
half-moon shape. To seal the empanadas, pinch the edges of the pastry
firmly together, then press down on the edges with the prongs
of a fork to finish.

Brush the empanadas with melted butter and bake in the oven for
15–18 minutes, or until golden and puffed. Serve hot or warm.

These are like devils-on-horseback, except I use a date instead of a prune. You must eat these while they are still warm and the dates are soft and moist from the still-hot bacon juices. As an alternative, try stuffing the dates with a small cube of blue cheese or mozzarella.

Dates Wrapped in Bacon

12 large (about 7 oz/200 g) dates (I use Medjool)

12 blanched almonds

6 (about 4 oz/125 g) bacon strips

Makes 12

Preheat the oven to 400°F/200°C. Line a baking sheet with foil.

Using a small knife, make a slit down one side of each date and remove the pit. Place one almond inside each date and push to close. Cut each strip of bacon in half through the middle and wrap one piece of bacon around each date. Use a cocktail stick or wooden toothpick to secure the bacon in place.

Put the wrapped dates on the baking sheet and cook in the preheated oven for 12–15 minutes, turning once, until the bacon is golden brown and crispy. Serve warm.

This recipe has Moorish influences coming through, with saffron and cinnamon being important flavors in the dish. If you like, you can use baby eggplants—this just becomes a little more fiddly when scooping out the eggplant flesh. Likewise, this filling can be used to stuff peppers, hollowed-out zucchini halves, or tomatoes—just adjust the cooking time depending on the vegetable you choose.

Eggplants Stuffed with Saffron Ground Lamb

1 tablespoon extra virgin olive oil

1 medium onion, peeled and finely chopped

14 oz/400 g ground lamb

¾ cup/200 ml passata (crushed tomatoes), or 7 oz/200 g can chopped tomatoes

½–1 teaspoon ground cinnamon

2 pinches of saffron threads

¾ cup/100 g stuffed green olives, of your choice, roughly chopped

4 small eggplants, 4–5 oz/125–150 g each

Makes 8 tapas-sized portions

Heat the olive oil in a large, nonstick skillet and sauté the onion for 2–3 minutes, or until soft and translucent but not browned. Add the ground lamb and cook, breaking it up, for 7–10 minutes, or until browned and the juices have evaporated.

Stir in the passata or tomatoes, the cinnamon, saffron, and olives and continue to simmer for a further 10–12 minutes.

While the meat mixture is cooking, preheat the oven to 400°F/200°C and prepare the eggplants. Cut each in half lengthwise and scoop out the flesh. Finely chop the flesh and add to the meat mixture for at least the last 5 minutes of cooking. Place the eggplant shells, cut-side up, on a baking sheet.

When the meat is cooked, fill the eggplant shells with the meat mixture and bake for 12–15 minutes, or until browned and the eggplant is soft. Serve hot, warm or cold.

The best chorizo contains as much as 95 percent pork along with salt, garlic, and paprika to give it its pronounced red color. It is cured either to a hard sausage consistency, to be sliced and eaten as it is, or to a softer consistency to use in cooking. The variety to choose for this tapa is the one that has not been completely cured and still requires cooking before eating. Depending on your preference, you can choose from mild, sweet, or spicy varieties.

Chorizo in Red Wine

3 (about 11 oz/300 g) cooking chorizo sausages, sliced into 1 inch/2.5 cm chunks

Heat a large, nonstick skillet and add the chorizo. Sauté for 3–4 minutes, or until the juices start to release and the chorizo starts to brown.

3½ tablespoons Rioja, or other red wine, or use sherry or Madeira

When the chorizo is crispy and golden, add the wine, increase the heat and sauté for a further couple of minutes until the juices start to caramelize and thicken.

Serves 4–6 as part of a selection of tapas

Serve immediately with cocktail sticks or wooden toothpicks.

For a more succulent and tender result, buy mini-chicken
fillets rather than chopping chicken breasts into smaller pieces.
The eggplants add a subtle meaty-like texture to this dish.

Mini Mediterranean Chicken Fillets

1 large eggplant

1 tablespoon extra
virgin olive oil

400 g/14 oz (about 8)
mini-chicken fillets, or
chicken breasts

1 teaspoon Spanish
hot smoked paprika

1 cup/250 g passata
(crushed tomatoes)

¾ cup/100 g
pimiento-stuffed
green olives

*Serves 4–6 as part of
a selection of tapas*

Preheat the oven to 400°F/200°C. Rub the eggplant with about
1 teaspoon of the olive oil and bake in the oven for 25–30 minutes, or
until soft and cooked. Remove from the oven and set aside until cool
enough to handle, then peel the eggplant and chop into large chunks.
Reduce the oven temperature to 350°F/180°C.

Meanwhile, if using chicken breasts, slice each one into 3–4 pieces.
Heat the remaining oil in a large, nonstick skillet and cook the chicken
for 2–3 minutes until golden brown. Add the paprika and stir to
combine, then add the passata, eggplant, and olives and cook for a
further 2–3 minutes.

Transfer to an ovenproof dish and cook in the oven for 15 minutes.
Serve hot or warm.

A Galician empanada is just one large pie cut into wedges, rather than individual crescents—somewhat like a calzone, except it's made using pastry. If you have the time, then make your own pastry—there's nothing more rewarding!

Galician-Style Chicken Empanada

1 quantity Empanada Pastry (see page 31), or 1 lb 10 oz/750 g bought puff pastry

2 tablespoons extra virgin olive oil

1 onion, peeled and finely chopped

1 red bell pepper, seeded and finely diced

1 teaspoon cumin seeds

14 oz/400 g chicken breasts, roughly chopped into small pieces

1–2 teaspoons harissa (optional)

½–1 teaspoon fine salt

1 small bunch of fresh cilantro, chopped

all-purpose flour, for dusting

Makes 12 tapas-sized portions

Prepare the pastry as on page 31 and refrigerate until ready to assemble.

Heat the olive oil in a large, nonstick skillet and sauté the onion for 3–4 minutes, or until translucent and soft. Add the diced bell pepper and cumin seeds and sauté for a further minute. Increase the heat, add the chicken and continue cooking, stirring frequently, until the chicken is cooked—this will take 5–7 minutes. Stir in the harissa paste and salt during the last few minutes of cooking. Stir in the cilantro and set aside to cool completely.

When you are ready to assemble the empanada, preheat the oven to 425°F/220°C. Roll the pastry out on a lightly floured surface to one large rectangle, about ¼ inch/5 mm thick, and cut around a plate, about 30 cm/12 inches in diameter, to give you two equal-sized circles. Place one on a large, lightly floured baking sheet. Spread the filling over evenly, then place the second circle on top. Brush the edge with a little water and, using your fingers, crimp around the edges to seal.

Bake in the oven for 15–20 minutes, or until golden brown. Leave to cool slightly, then cut into wedges to serve. This can also be served cold.

Pork spare ribs are one of the least expensive cuts from the pig and make a great tapa that seems to appeal to young and old alike. Try cooking these on the barbecue for a slightly smoky and charred taste, but have lots of paper towels handy for all those sticky fingers!

To me, these pork skewers, with a splash of sherry and a dash of paprika, sum up the essence of Spanish tapas. Simple yet hearty, they are a party pleaser every time and are delicious served with a glass of chilled beer or fino sherry.

Sherry-Marinated Pork Ribs

1 lb 2 oz/500 g (12–15) mini pork ribs

For the marinade

2 tablespoons honey, plus extra to drizzle

1 tablespoon extra virgin olive oil

3½ tablespoons dry sherry

1 teaspoon Spanish hot smoked paprika

2 tablespoons tomato paste

1 garlic clove, peeled and crushed

2 sprigs fresh thyme, leaves removed

Serves 4–6 as part of a selection of tapas

If the ribs are still in a rack, cut them into individual ribs, place in a large, nonmetallic bowl and set aside.

Combine all the marinade ingredients in a bowl and pour over the ribs. Mix well to coat, then cover and refrigerate for 4–24 hours, turning occasionally.

When you are ready to cook, preheat the oven to 425°F/220°C. Remove the ribs from the marinade and place in a single layer on a baking sheet. Drizzle all over with a little extra honey. Cook in the oven for 18–20 minutes, turning and basting once or twice, until sticky and slightly charred. Serve immediately.

Marinated Pork Skewers (Pinchos Morunos)

1½ lb/675 g pork fillet, cut into approximately 1¼ inch/3 cm cubes

12 short bamboo skewers, soaked in water for 2–24 hours

For the marinade

1 teaspoon cumin seeds

1 teaspoon fennel seeds

½ teaspoon Spanish hot smoked paprika

1 garlic clove, peeled and crushed

2 tablespoons extra virgin olive oil

1 tablespoon fino (dry) sherry

Serves 4–6 as part of a selection of tapas

Combine all the marinade ingredients in a large bowl. Add the pork and toss well to coat, then cover and leave to marinate for at least 1 hour, or up to 24 hours.

When ready to cook, preheat the broiler to hot. Thread 3–4 cubes of pork on to each skewer and place on a foil-lined baking sheet. Broil for 5 minutes on one side, then turn and broil for a further 3–4 minutes, or until golden, aromatic and the pork is cooked through.

Serve warm.

The word "sherry" has become so generic over the decades that the distinctive characteristics of many noble styles such as fino, manzanilla, amontillado, oloroso, and Pedro Ximenez have often been disregarded. It is important to familiarize yourself with the spectrum of flavors that each style contains so that you can add a new dimension to your cooking. Dry varieties such as fino and Pedro Ximenez work particularly well in this dish.

Sweet Sherry Onions with Morcilla

1 tablespoon butter

1 tablespoon extra virgin olive oil

1 bay leaf

11 oz/300 g baby onions, peeled

2 tablespoons fino (dry) or Pedro Ximenez sherry

1 tablespoon balsamic vinegar

1 tablespoon superfine sugar

1 small bunch fresh flat-leaf parsley, finely chopped

7 oz/200 g morcilla (blood sausage) or mini cooking chorizo sausages

salt and freshly ground black pepper

Serves 4–6 as part of a selection of tapas

Heat the butter and olive oil in a large, nonstick skillet until the butter has melted. Add the bay leaf and onions and cook for about 4–5 minutes, stirring regularly, until the onions are golden all over. Add the sherry, vinegar, and sugar, reduce the heat and cook for a further 5–7 minutes, or until the onions are caramelized and soft. Remove from the heat, season to taste and stir in the parsley, then set aside while you prepare the morcilla.

If using large sausages, cut the morcilla or chorizo into about ½ inch/ 1 cm thick slices; keep mini sausages whole.

Heat a clean skillet to medium hot, add the sausages and cook, turning frequently, until they are golden, cooked, and the oils have run out— 5–7 minutes. Add the onions to the pan and cook together for a further 2–3 minutes. Serve warm.

Fish & Seafood

Serve these with good crusty bread—to me, the best part of eating mussels is soaking up the delicious juices. Saffron, the stigma of a species of crocus, is the most expensive spice in the world so I've made it optional, but do use it if you can as it gives a lovely color.

I had a similar dish to this in one of my favorite restaurants in Auckland. There, the Asian-inspired mussels were baked with wasabi. My version uses garlic instead and is finished with a little chili. Try to use New Zealand green-lipped mussels, which are larger than other ones.

Mussels in Wine, Tomato and Chile Sauce

Alioli and Chili-Broiled Mussels

2¼ lb/1 kg mussels

2 tablespoons extra virgin olive oil

1 onion, peeled and finely chopped

½ teaspoon crushed dried chile flakes

a pinch of saffron threads (optional)

2 tablespoons tomato paste

5 tablespoons red wine

a small handful of fresh flat-leaf parsley, chopped

salt and freshly ground black pepper

Serves 4–6 as part of a selection of tapas

Wash the mussels thoroughly, remove the beards and discard any mussels that are broken or remain open when tapped sharply.

Heat the olive oil in a large saucepan and sauté the onion for 2–3 minutes, or until soft and translucent but not browned. Add the chile flakes, saffron, and tomato paste and mix well. Add the red wine, then stir in the mussels, cover the pan and steam, shaking regularly, for 4–6 minutes, or until all the mussels are open. Discard any mussels that do not open. Stir in the parsley, season to taste and serve immediately.

12 cooked, green-lipped mussels, in the half shell

12 tablespoons Alioli (see page 19), or garlic mayonnaise

2 tablespoons smoked chili jam, or sweet chili sauce

Serves 4–6 as part of a selection of tapas

Preheat the grill to hot. Place the mussels in their half shell, flesh-side up, on a baking tray. Spread 1 tablespoon of alioli or mayonnaise over each mussel, to completely cover the flesh, then place ½ teaspoon of chili jam or sweet chili sauce on top.

Place under the broiler and cook for 3–5 minutes, or until bubbling, slightly golden and each mussel is hot. Serve immediately with cocktail sticks or wooden toothpicks.

If you have it available, use fresh white crab meat instead of canned. However, canned will also give you a very good result. The slightly spongy texture is typical of many fish balls I have tasted in Spain.

Crab and Lemon Balls

1 large egg, beaten

1 tablespoon fino (dry) sherry

a pinch of hot chili powder

1 tablespoon mayonnaise

1 sprig fresh rosemary, finely chopped

zest of 1 lemon

6 oz/170 g can white crab meat, drained

1½ cups/75 g fresh breadcrumbs

about 1 tablespoon all-purpose flour, for dusting

4 tablespoons extra virgin olive oil

salt and freshly ground black pepper

Serves 4–6 as part of a selection of tapas

Whisk the egg, sherry, chili powder, mayonnaise, rosemary, and lemon zest together in a bowl. Season well, then stir in the crab meat and breadcrumbs to form a firm but still wet mixture that can be shaped into balls. If the mixture is too wet, add more breadcrumbs.

Using dampened hands, shape the mixture into 12 heaped tablespoon-sized balls and place on a lightly floured plate. Chill, covered, for at least 30 minutes, or up to 12 hours.

Heat the olive oil in a large skillet to medium heat. Add the crab balls and cook for 4–6 minutes, turning frequently to keep their round shape. The balls should be golden brown and cooked through.

Drain on paper towels and serve warm with cocktail sticks or wooden toothpicks.

The Galician region in the northwest of Spain is famous for its shell-fish and locally produced cider. I've combined these two ingredients to make a true Galician delicacy. These are delicious with a salsa verde or Sweet Chili and Red Pepper Salsa (see page 29) for dipping.

72 Scallop Fritters in Cider Batter

⅔ cup/75 g all-purpose flour

1 egg, separated

1 tablespoon extra virgin olive oil

5 tablespoons cider at room temperature

4 cups/1 liter vegetable oil

11 oz/300 g scallops, halved if large

salt and freshly ground black pepper

lemon wedges, to serve

Serves 4 as part of a selection of tapas

Sift the flour into a medium-sized bowl and stir in ¼ teaspoon of salt. Make a well in the center and set aside.

In a separate bowl, whisk the egg yolk, olive oil, and cider together. Pour the liquid mixture into the flour well and stir, using a whisk, until just combined. Cover and refrigerate for 1 hour.

Whisk the egg white in a clean, grease-free bowl until stiff peaks form, then gently fold into the cider batter until just combined.

Heat the vegetable oil in a large, heavy-bottomed saucepan to 375°F/190°C, or until a small cube of bread turns golden in about 30 seconds. If the scallops are large, remove the orange roes and cook them separately. Season the scallops (and roes) with salt and pepper.

When the oil is hot enough, using a spoon, dip the scallops into the batter, one at a time, and gently lower into the oil. Cook in batches for 1–2 minutes, or until golden brown and the scallop is cooked through.

Remove with a slotted spoon and drain on paper towels, then serve hot with lemon wedges on the side.

Best cooked on the barbecue and lightly charred on the outside, these little fish are good served with some crusty sourdough bread and a few broiled tomatoes for the ultimate in tapas combinations.

Many people think canned whole tomatoes are inferior to fresh tomatoes, but they couldn't be more wrong. In fact, it is the best-quality tomatoes that are usually selected for the canning process, so they should be sweet, juicy, and full of flavor.

Grilled Sardines

Clams in Cherry Tomato Sauce

12 small sardines

2 tablespoons lemon juice

2 tablespoons extra virgin olive oil

1 teaspoon dried crushed chiles

1 teaspoon dried oregano

sea salt

lemon wedges, to serve

Serves 4–6 as part of a selection of tapas

Make 2–3 shallow slashes on both sides of each sardine and set aside in a shallow dish.

Combine the lemon juice, olive oil, crushed chiles and oregano in a bowl and pour over the sardines. Leave to marinate for at least 30 minutes, or up to 12 hours.

Preheat a barbecue or griddle pan to hot and cook the sardines for 3–4 minutes on each side, or until opaque through and crispy on the outside. Serve sprinkled with sea salt, with lemon wedges on the side.

2¼ lb/1 kg clams, left to sit in cold, salted water for about 2 hours to expel any sand or grit

2 tablespoons extra virgin olive oil

1 small onion, peeled and finely chopped

1 fennel bulb, finely chopped

2 garlic cloves, peeled and chopped

2 tablespoons fino (dry) sherry

14 oz/400 g can baby cherry tomatoes in juice

a small handful of torn fresh flat-leaf parsley

sea salt and freshly ground black pepper

Serves 4–6 as part of a selection of tapas

Wash the clams, discarding any that are cracked, broken or will not close when tapped sharply.

Heat the olive oil in a large, heavy-bottomed saucepan. Add the onion and fennel and cook slowly for 2–3 minutes until cooked but not browned.

Add the garlic, sherry, clams, and tomatoes, with their juice, and stir, then cover the pan and cook the clams for a further 2–3 minutes, shaking the pan occasionally, or until most of the clams are open.

Stir in the parsley and season to taste, then turn out into a serving dish and discard any clams that have not opened.

Serve immediately with bread on the side to mop up any juices.

Pork goes particularly well with fish and shellfish and this dish is no exception. These tidy little skewers are the perfect tapa and are exceptionally good when cooked on the barbecue to give a slightly smoky and charred taste.

Fresh seafood with a squeeze of lemon juice is simplicity at its best. These not only taste good but they look great too.

Shrimp and Chorizo Skewers

Barbecued Shrimp and Scallop Skewers

12 raw large shrimp, peeled (leave tails on if preferred) and deveined

1 tablespoon extra virgin olive oil

1 small bunch of fresh flat-leaf parsley, finely chopped

2 cooking chorizo sausages, about 5 oz/150 g each, cut into ¾ inch/1.5 cm thick slices

12 short bamboo skewers, soaked in water for as long as possible, up to 24 hours

Makes 12

Place the shrimp in a bowl with the olive oil and parsley and mix to coat.

Place a slice of chorizo into the crook of each shrimp and thread on to a skewer.

Cook the skewers on a preheated barbecue or under a hot broiler for 5–7 minutes, turning once or twice, or until cooked and slightly charred. Serve immediately.

12 small scallops

4 scallions, trimmed and each cut into three pieces, about 1¾ inches/4 cm long

12 raw large shrimp, peeled (leave tails on) and deveined

extra virgin olive oil

sea salt and freshly ground black pepper

12 bamboo skewers, soaked in water for as long as possible, up to 24 hours

To serve

lemon wedges

Alioli (see page 19)

Makes 12

Using a small knife or your fingers, remove any membrane or hard white muscle from the scallops. Skewer one scallop on to each skewer, followed by a piece of scallion. Curl up the shrimp so that the ends meet and thread on to the skewer. Brush the skewers lightly with olive oil and sprinkle with a little salt and black pepper.

Cook the skewers on a preheated barbecue or under a hot broiler for 1–2 minutes on each side, or until the seafood is just cooked. Serve hot with lemon wedges and alioli for dipping.

These little morsels melt in your mouth and give you a punch of heat afterwards. Perfectly accompanied by a cooling citrus yogurt sauce, they go well with almost any selection of tapas and a chilled glass of white wine.

Blackened Salmon with Orange Yogurt Sauce

10 oz/300 g salmon fillet, skinned and boned

2 tablespoons vegetable oil

1 teaspoon dried thyme

1 teaspoon dried rosemary

1 teaspoon dried oregano

½ teaspoon Spanish sweet smoked paprika

½ teaspoon cayenne pepper

1 garlic clove, peeled and crushed

1 teaspoon cumin seeds, lightly toasted

1 teaspoon fine salt

For the citrus yoghurt

300 ml/½ pint thick, creamy yogurt

zest and juice of 1 orange

¼ cup/60 ml extra virgin olive oil

Serves 4 as part of a selection of tapas

Cut the prepared salmon fillet into 1 inch/2.5 cm cubes. Coat the salmon in 1 tablespoon of the vegetable oil and then set aside in a large dish.

Combine the thyme, rosemary, oregano, paprika, cayenne, garlic, cumin seeds, and salt in a small bowl. Generously coat the salmon cubes in the spice mixture and leave to sit while you prepare the yogurt.

Put the yogurt, orange zest and juice, and the olive oil in a bowl and, using a small whisk, combine, then set aside.

Heat the remaining vegetable oil in a large, nonstick skillet and cook the salmon for 3–4 minutes, turning frequently until golden all over and cooked through.

Serve warm with cocktail sticks or wooden toothpicks and the yogurt sauce for dipping.

The simplicity of this dish is what makes it so special. Crisp lettuce with salty anchovies, finished with nothing but the finest of extra virgin olive oils—what more could you want?

These really should come under the recipe for Banderillas (see page 20), but I thought they deserved recognition of their own. Sticky sweet onions wrapped in sharp anchovies are bliss.

Baby Romaine Lettuce with Anchovies

Caramelized Onions Wrapped in Anchovies

2 baby romaine lettuces

12 anchovies, canned or marinated

extra virgin olive oil

freshly ground black pepper

Serves 4–6 as part of a selection of tapas

Remove and discard the outer leaves from the lettuce and chop the lettuce in half lengthwise. Then chop each half into three lengthwise wedges.

Place each wedge, pointy side up, on a serving plate and position 1 anchovy down its length. Drizzle generously with olive oil and season with black pepper.

1 quantity Sweet Sherry Onions (see page 67), omitting the morcilla or chorizo

about 18 anchovies marinated in vinegar and olive oil

Makes 18

Make the recipe for the onions and allow them to cool completely. (This recipe should give you about 18 baby onions.)

Wrap an anchovy around the circumference of each onion and secure it with a cocktail stick. Serve cold.

You will find a lot of deep-fried food in Spanish cooking and the use of oil is prolific. This is one dish you will see on the menu of almost every restaurant within a five-mile radius of the coast. Make sure you use very fresh squid and fry for only long enough to just cook it.

Deep-Fried Squid Rings

1½ lb/675 g
fresh squid

vegetable oil, for
deep-frying

⅞ cup/100 g
all-purpose flour,
for coating

2 eggs, beaten with
1 tablespoon of water

2 cups/100 g
breadcrumbs

lemon wedges,
to serve

*Serves 4 as part of a
selection of tapas*

First prepare the squid. Pull out and discard the head and the attached intestines from the tube-like body and remove and discard the long, thin cartilage. Cut off the wings from the body and, using your fingers, pull the skin away and discard. Rinse the tubes under running cold water, then pat dry using paper towels. Cut the tubes into rings about ¼ inch/ 5 mm thick.

Heat the vegetable oil in a large, heavy-bottomed saucepan to 375°F/ 190°C, or until a small cube of bread turns golden in about 30 seconds.

Put the flour, egg, and breadcrumbs in three separate bowls and line them up in order. Dredge the squid rings in the flour, then dip them in the egg mixture and, finally, coat with the breadcrumbs. Deep-fry the squid for 1–1½ minutes, or until golden. Do not over-cook them or the squid will turn tough.

Remove with a slotted spoon and drain on paper towels, then serve immediately with lemon wedges on the side.

Ask your fish seller for tenderized baby octopus, or you will have to go through the rigorous task of tenderizing it yourself—this involves throwing it forcefully at a hard surface 30–40 times and is not a pleasant task.

If I put a plate of these in front of my partner, he'll devour them within minutes. I always serve them with crusty bread to mop up the lovely marinade. They are a useful standby to keep in the refrigerator and can be incorporated into many tapas, such as wrapped around baby onions.

Marinated Octopus and Fennel Salad

Marinated Anchovies

1.5 kg/3½ lb tenderized baby octopus

8 cups/2 liters water

½ cup/100 ml white wine vinegar

3 bay leaves

1 teaspoon black peppercorns

1 fennel bulb, shaved

5 tablespoons extra virgin olive oil

juice of 2 lemons

1 tablespoon chopped fresh dill

salt and freshly ground black pepper

lemon wedges, to serve (optional)

Serves 4–6 as part of a selection of tapas

Clean the octopus and remove and discard the head.

Pour the water into a large saucepan and bring to a boil. Add the vinegar, bay leaves, peppercorns, and octopus and bring back to a boil, then boil for 20–25 minutes, or until the octopus is tender. (Test by cutting a bit off and tasting it.)

Remove the octopus from the saucepan and rinse it under running cold water, discarding any skin. Cut the octopus into bite-sized chunks and put into a large bowl. Add the fennel, olive oil, lemon juice, and dill and mix well. Cover and leave to marinate overnight in the refrigerator.

Just before serving, season to taste and serve with lemon wedges, if liked.

3½ oz/100 g anchovy fillets, drained

1 small red onion, peeled and very finely chopped

1 small bunch of fresh flat-leaf parsley, roughly chopped

1 tablespoon capers, rinsed and roughly chopped

1 tablespoon red wine vinegar

4 tablespoons extra virgin olive oil

Serves 4–6 as part of a selection of tapas

Place the drained anchovies flat on a serving plate. Put the onion, parsley, and capers in a small bowl, add the vinegar and olive oil and stir to combine.

Pour this marinade over the anchovies and leave to marinate for at least 30 minutes, or up to 48 hours.

I think fresh, succulent oysters are best eaten raw. However, if you prefer, just before serving you can put the dressed oysters under a preheated broiler for 1–2 minutes. Cava is a sparkling Spanish white wine, but you can use any sparkling white wine if you can't find it.

Oysters with Cava Dressing

12 oysters, in their half shell

1 small red onion, peeled and very finely chopped

1 tablespoon sherry vinegar, or cider vinegar

3½ tablespoons Cava, or other sparkling white wine

freshly ground black pepper

To serve

sourdough bread

lemon wedges

Makes 12 tapas-sized portions

Arrange the oysters in a single layer on a large serving platter. Place the onion, vinegar, Cava, and black pepper in a small bowl and stir to combine.

Pour the dressing over the oysters and leave to marinate for up to 15 minutes before serving.

Serve with some sourdough bread, generously buttered, and some lemon wedges.

I ate these in Valencia under a laden orange tree. Even now, the smell of orange blossom takes me back to this one dish. The garlic chile butter that remains after you've devoured all the shrimp is great mopped up with some crusty bread.

Baked Chile-Butter Shrimp

2 tablespoons extra virgin olive oil

¼ stick/30 g salted butter

1 large red chile, seeded and finely chopped

1 garlic clove, peeled and crushed

300 g/11 oz peeled and deveined raw large shrimp

1 small bunch of fresh flat-leaf parsley, finely chopped

sea salt

Serves 4 as part of a selection of tapas

Preheat the oven to 350°F/180°C. Heat the olive oil and butter in a small saucepan. Add the chopped chile and garlic and sauté for 2–3 minutes until cooked but not browned.

Put the shrimp in an ovenproof dish and pour over the butter mixture. Cook in the oven for 5–7 minutes, or until the shrimp are cooked.

Remove from the oven, sprinkle over the parsley and sea salt and serve hot.

There's nothing more satisfying than getting your fingers stuck into a bowl of whole barbecued shrimp. Prepare a dipping bowl of water and lemon wedges so that people can wash their hands before moving on to the next tapas dish.

Garlic and Tio Pepe Shrimp

2 tablespoons extra virgin olive oil

2 garlic cloves, peeled and finely chopped

1 large red chile, deseeded and finely chopped

4½ lb/2 kg raw unpeeled shrimp

2 tablespoons Tio Pepe, or other dry sherry

a small handful of chopped fresh flat-leaf parsley

Serves 4 as part of a selection of tapas

Heat the olive oil in a large, nonstick skillet. Add the garlic and chopped chile and sauté quickly but do not brown.

Increase the heat, add the shrimp and sherry and shake the pan over the heat until the shrimp turn pink and are cooked—2–3 minutes.

Remove from the heat, stir in the parsley and serve immediately.

Fresh squid quickly fried so that it melts in your mouth and served with garlic alioli is really a taste sensation that can't be surpassed.

Crispy Paprika-Salt Squid

14 oz/400 g prepared squid tubes

vegetable oil, for deep-frying

⅞ cup/100 g all-purpose flour

½ teaspoon Spanish hot smoked paprika

1 teaspoon salt

Alioli (see page 19)

Serves 4 as part of a selection of tapas

Rinse the squid under running cold water and pat dry using paper towels. Cut the tubes along one side to open them out. Using a sharp knife, lightly score the inside surface of each tube in a criss-cross pattern, making sure you do not cut right through. Then cut them into about 1¾ inch/4 cm pieces. Cut the tentacles, if you have them, into smaller bite-sized pieces.

Fill a heavy-bottomed saucepan with vegetable oil and heat to 375°F/190°C, or until a small cube of bread turns golden in about 30 seconds.

While the oil is heating, combine the flour, paprika, and salt in a bowl. Add the squid and mix until well coated. Shake off the squid and add to the oil in batches, cooking for 1–2 minutes each batch, or until golden, crispy, and cooked through.

Remove with a slotted spoon and drain on paper towels. Serve warm with alioli on the side.

To me, stuffed baby squid is a true taste of the Mediterranean. I have taken on more of the flavors of North Africa for this particular dish, but a nonmeat version using breadcrumbs, fresh herbs, and lemon is a favorite, too. These are also delicious charred on the barbecue.

Stuffed Baby Squid

1 tablespoon extra virgin olive oil

1 small onion, peeled and very finely chopped

1 garlic clove, peeled and crushed

½ teaspoon cayenne pepper

½ teaspoon Spanish sweet smoked paprika

1 teaspoon ground cumin

1 tablespoon tomato paste

1 teaspoon superfine sugar

7 oz/200 g ground pork

5 tablespoons white wine

1 tablespoon chopped fresh flat-leaf parsley

9 oz/250 g baby squid tubes, 2–2½ inches/ 5–6 cm long

all-purpose flour, for coating

oil, for shallow-frying

sea salt and freshly ground black pepper

Makes about 18

Heat the olive oil in a large, nonstick skillet. Add the onion, garlic, cayenne, paprika, and cumin and sauté until the onion is soft and translucent but not browned. Stir in the tomato paste and sugar, then increase the heat and add the ground pork. Using a wooden spoon, break up the meat and cook for about 5 minutes. Add the wine, then reduce the heat and cook for a further 10–12 minutes. Stir in the parsley and season accordingly. Leave to cool.

To prepare the squid, trim off the wide end of each tube to neaten. Rinse the squid and pat dry, inside and out, using paper towels. Fill the tubes with the cooled meat mixture—but do not overfill—and secure the ends with cocktail sticks or wooden toothpicks. Coat the squid in flour.

Heat the oil in a nonstick skillet and, when hot, shallow-fry the squid for 2–3 minutes, or until the squid is just cooked. Sprinkle with sea salt and serve hot.

Salt cod is whole, gutted cod that has been coated with coarse sea salt and left to hang and dry, thus preserving it. Make sure you soak the salt cod for at least the time specified in order to de-salt it thoroughly. If you can, buy center cuts of the fillet, which are the fatter and meatier ones. As an alternative, use 14 oz/400 g fresh cod fillets and season to taste.

Salt Cod Croquettes

14 oz/400 g salt cod, soaked in water for 24–36 hours and water changed 3–4 times

3 cups/750 ml milk

3 bay leaves

1 teaspoon black peppercorns

zest of 1 lemon, cut into large strips using a potato peeler

1 lb 2 oz/500 g mealy potatoes, such as Yukon Gold, peeled and cut into chunks

3½ tablespoons all-purpose flour, plus extra for dusting

1 large bunch of fresh flat-leaf parsley or cilantro, finely chopped

3 cups/750 ml vegetable or sunflower oil

freshly ground black pepper

To serve

lemon wedges

Alioli (see page 19)

Makes about 20

Drain the salt cod and place in a saucepan with the milk, bay leaves, peppercorns, and lemon zest and bring to the boil. Reduce the heat and simmer for about 5 minutes, or until the fish flakes easily. Remove the salt cod from the milk and set aside to cool.

Pass the milk through a strainer and return the milk to the saucepan. Add the potatoes and bring to a boil, then reduce the heat and simmer for about 15 minutes, or until soft.

While the potatoes are cooking, pull the cod apart, discarding any bones or skin, and set aside in a bowl.

When the potatoes are cooked, drain and add to the cod along with the flour, parsley, and a good grind of black pepper. Using a fork, mash all the ingredients together until well combined. Using a spoon and your hand, shape the mixture into croquettes, about walnut-size, and set aside on a lightly floured tray or board.

Heat the vegetable or sunflower oil in a heavy-bottomed saucepan to 375°F/190°C, or until a small cube of bread turns golden in about 30 seconds.

Cook the croquettes in batches for 2–3 minutes each batch, or until hot through and golden in color.

Remove with a slotted spoon and drain on paper towels. Serve warm with lemon wedges and alioli on the side.

Whitebait from UK and Mediterranean waters differs from the whitebait you'll find in my homeland New Zealand or smelt in the US. If this large variety of smelt or whitebait is unavailable, use whole anchovies or small sardines—just adjust the cooking time according to size.

Fried Smelt

200 g/7 oz fresh smelt or whitebait

scant ½ cup/ 100 ml milk

all-purpose flour, for coating

vegetable or sunflower oil, for deep-frying

sea salt

lemon wedges, to serve

Serves 4–6 as part of a selection of tapas

Dip the fish in the milk, then coat them in flour.

Heat the vegetable or sunflower oil in a large, heavy-bottomed saucepan to 375°F/190°C, or until a small cube of bread turns golden in about 30 seconds.

Deep-fry the smelt in the oil for 1–2 minutes, or until golden and crispy. Drain on paper towels and sprinkle with salt. Serve hot with lemon wedges on the side.

This Galician specialty sauce is a favorite with poached fish. I like to use halibut, a firm white fish that holds its shape when poached. Anglerfish works well, too, but you can choose a more flaky fish such as cod or haddock, if you prefer.

Poached Halibut with Paprika Sauce

14 oz/400 g halibut fillets, cut into large chunky pieces

½ teaspoon black peppercorns

4 garlic cloves, peeled and cut into quarters

2 bay leaves

scant ½ cup extra virgin olive oil

1–2 teaspoons Spanish hot or sweet smoked paprika

1 tablespoon white wine vinegar

4 tablespoons hot fish stock, or fish cooking liquid

Serves 4 as part of a selection of tapas

Put the halibut and peppercorns in a small skillet or saucepan and just cover with boiling water. Bring to a gentle simmer and then simmer for 3–4 minutes, or until the fish is just cooked. Using a slotted spoon, remove from the liquid and transfer to several small serving dishes, or one large dish.

Put the garlic, the bay leaves, and the olive oil in a saucepan and cook gently, without letting the garlic color, until hot.

Remove from the heat and stir in the paprika, vinegar, and hot fish stock or fish cooking liquid. Stir to combine, then pour the liquid evenly over the fish and serve immediately, garnished with the bay leaves from the sauce.

Cold fish—yuk! That's what I thought, too, when a similar dish was placed in front of me, but it's actually delicious. And the great thing is that it can be made in advance with no last-minute cooking. These fish medallions are incredibly fragrant and full of flavor and will simply melt in your mouth. The recipe does, however, require a firm fish that can withstand the long marinating.

Spanish Anglerfish Medallions

For the marinade

6 tablespoons extra virgin olive oil

1 large onion, peeled and finely sliced

1 teaspoon cumin seeds

a large pinch of saffron threads

1 cinnamon stick, broken in half

1 garlic clove, peeled and crushed

1 sprig fresh thyme

zest and juice of 1 orange

3½ tablespoons dry sherry

3½ tablespoons cider vinegar

2 tablespoons honey

2 tablespoons extra virgin olive oil

1½ lb/675 g anglerfish fillets, cut into 1 inch/2.5 cm chunks

⅞ cup seasoned all-purpose flour

salt and freshly ground black pepper

Serves 6 as part of a selection of tapas

To make the marinade, heat 4 tablespoons of the olive oil in a large, nonstick skillet. Add the onion, cumin seeds, saffron, and cinnamon stick and sauté for 3–4 minutes, or until the onion is softened but not browned. Add the garlic and thyme and sauté for a further 2–3 minutes. Add the orange zest and juice, sherry, vinegar and honey and bring to a boil. Boil for about 2 minutes, then remove from the heat, taste and season and transfer to a small bowl.

Wipe out the pan, add the remaining 2 tablespoons olive oil and place over medium heat. Coat the fish in the seasoned flour and cook in batches until golden and cooked through.

Transfer the fish to a serving plate and pour over the marinade. Leave to cool, then cover and refrigerate for up to 24 hours. Remove from the refrigerator 30 minutes before serving.

You can make these small, medium or large—whatever the occasion demands. As a tapa, they are best kept small so that you can pick them up and eat them in one mouthful. For a main meal, make four large fish cakes and serve with a green salad and lots of lemon wedges.

Salmon, Caper, and Dill Fish Cakes

11 oz/300 g salmon fillet, skinned and boned

1 tablespoon extra virgin olive oil

1 small onion, peeled and very finely chopped

¾ cup/150 g mashed potato

2 tablespoons capers, rinsed and roughly chopped

1½ tablespoons chopped dill

⅞ cup/100 g all-purpose flour, for coating

1 egg, beaten

2 cups/100 g fresh breadcrumbs, for coating

¼ stick/about 30 g butter

salt and freshly ground black pepper

lemon wedges, to serve

Serves 6 as part of a selection of tapas

Preheat the oven to 350°F/180°C. Put the salmon on to an oiled baking sheet and cook in the oven for 8–10 minutes, or until it is cooked and flakes when broken with a fork.

Heat the olive oil in a small saucepan and cook the onion for 3–4 minutes, or until softened but not browned.

Combine the mashed potato, onion, and flaked salmon in a large bowl and, using a fork, mix well. Stir in the capers and dill. Taste and season accordingly. Refrigerate the mixture for at least 1 hour.

Put the flour, egg, and breadcrumbs in three separate bowls and line them up in that order. Roll the mixture into tablespoon-sized balls and flatten with the palm of your hand. Coat each fish cake in the flour, then dip in the beaten egg and, finally, roll each in the breadcrumbs to coat.

Heat half the butter in a large skillet and cook half the fish cakes for 2–3 minutes on each side, or until hot through and golden brown. Repeat with the remaining butter and fish cakes.

Serve hot or warm with lemon wedges.

This Catalonian specialty uses ingredients such as almonds and saffron which were brought to Spain by the Moors as early as the 7th century. Almond trees now grow prolifically in the area. The sauce is basically a romesco sauce without peppers and with saffron added.

White Fish in an Almond, Saffron, and Bread Sauce

4 tablespoons extra virgin olive oil

½ cup/50 g blanched almonds

2 garlic cloves, peeled and sliced

2 slices of fresh thick white bread, crusts removed and roughly torn

3½ tablespoons fino (dry) sherry

a pinch of saffron threads

1 onion, peeled and finely chopped

1 large beef tomato, finely diced

⅔ cup/150 ml boiling water

1 lb 2 oz/500 g skinless cod, anglerfish or other firm white fish, cut into about 20 cubes

salt and freshly ground black pepper

fresh flat-leaf parsley, to serve (optional)

Serves 4 as part of a selection of tapas

Heat 3 tablespoons of the olive oil in a large, nonstick skillet and fry the almonds for 2–3 minutes. Add the garlic and bread and continue frying until they are lightly golden and most of the oil has been absorbed. This will only take a few more minutes.

Remove from the heat and place in a food processor with the sherry and saffron, then whiz to a paste.

Cook the onion in the remaining oil for 3–4 minutes, or until translucent but not browned. Stir in the almond mixture, tomato, and boiling water and simmer for about 3 minutes. Season the sauce to your liking, then add the fish, cover and cook for a further 3–5 minutes, stirring once, or until the fish is just cooked.

Serve hot, sprinkled with flat-leaf parsley, if liked.

Ask your fish seller to fillet the sardines—if you're not a skilled hand with the filleting knife, it can be a fiddly job. You need to start preparing these at least three days before you want to eat them.

Marinated Sardines with Shaved Fennel

1 cup/100 g sea salt

8 large sardines, filleted

½ cup/125 ml cider vinegar

2 cups/500 ml water

3 bay leaves

1 onion, peeled and chopped into chunks

1 fennel bulb, cut into chunks

½ teaspoon black peppercorns

½ cup/125 ml extra virgin olive oil

To serve

1 fennel bulb, very finely shaved or sliced

salt and freshly ground black pepper

Serves 4 as part of a selection of tapas

Sprinkle half the sea salt into a large, nonmetallic dish (glass or plastic is best) and place the filleted sardines on top. Sprinkle over the remaining salt, cover and refrigerate for about 24 hours.

Put all the remaining ingredients, except the olive oil, into a saucepan and bring to a boil, then reduce the heat and simmer for 30 minutes. Take off the heat and leave to cool completely.

When the sardines have had 24 hours in salt, wipe off the salt and put them back into a clean, nonmetallic dish. Pour over the cooled vinegar liquid and refrigerate for a further 24 hours.

Remove the sardines from the vinegar and again place in a clean, nonmetallic dish. Cover with the olive oil and refrigerate for at least 24 hours, or up to 1 week.

Serve the marinated sardines topped with very finely shaved or sliced fennel and seasoned with salt and black pepper.

These succulent, juicy fritters are simple to make. Chickpea flour, also known as gram flour, has an unmistakable yellow color and a matte finish. It has a dry, earthy aroma and slightly nutty taste. If you can't find it, substitute potato or rice flour, or just use all-purpose flour.

Shrimp Fritters

½–1 teaspoon
chili powder

⅞ cup/100 g chickpea
flour, or gram flour

½ cup/60 g
all-purpose flour

a generous
pinch of salt

about ¾ cup/200 ml
cold water

13 oz/400 g raw,
peeled shrimp,
deveined and roughly
chopped

1 garlic clove,
peeled and crushed

a small handful of
fresh flat-leaf parsley,
chopped

olive oil, for frying

lemon wedges,
to serve

Makes 15

Put the chili powder, chickpea or gram flour, the all-purpose flour and salt in a large bowl. Slowly add the water, using just enough to make a pouring batter, ensuring that all the flour is mixed in.

Gently stir in the shrimp, garlic, and parsley.

Heat about 1 tablespoon of olive oil in a large, nonstick skillet. Fry large spoonfuls of the shrimp batter in batches until cooked and golden brown on both sides—3–4 minutes. Replenish the oil as necessary between batches. Drain on paper towels.

Serve warm with lemon wedges on the side.

Piquillo peppers (also called pimiento) are peppers that have been cooked and peeled and are ready-prepared to be used in dishes. They are widely available these days and should easily be found at your supermarket in either cans or jars.

Depending on the time of year, these can be served hot or cold. Either way they are delicious, and they also work well as a party canapé. For a completely vegetarian option, make the olive paste without anchovies.

Walnut and Cheese-Stuffed Piquillos

1 cup/100 g fresh walnuts, roughly chopped

3 oz/75 g soft goat's cheese

2 tablespoons chopped soft herbs, such as parsley, tarragon, chives

zest of 1 small lemon

5 oz/150 g can small piquillo peppers (about 12 in a can)

freshly ground black pepper

Makes about 12

Combine the walnuts, goat's cheese, herbs, and lemon zest in a bowl, then season with black pepper.

Place the peppers on a flat surface and spoon a heaped teaspoonful of the mixture into each one. Transfer to a serving plate and chill.

Serve cold.

Cherry Tomatoes Stuffed with Olive Paste

12 cherry tomatoes

4 tablespoons Black Olive Paste (see page 15)

extra virgin olive oil

flat-leaf parsley, to serve

Makes 24

If you are serving these warm, preheat the oven to 350°F/180°C. Halve the cherry tomatoes horizontally and, using a teaspoon, carefully scoop out the pulp and discard it.

Place the tomato halves, cut-side up, on a baking sheet, or on a serving dish. Spoon ½ teaspoon of olive paste into each tomato half and drizzle with olive oil. If serving warm, bake in the oven for 5–7 minutes, or until hot through and the tomato is cooked but not yet collapsing. Remove from the oven.

Garnish each tomato half with a sprig of parsley and a good grind of black pepper, then serve.

These can easily become a vegetarian tapa by taking out the prosciutto (ham). Adjust the seasoning accordingly and hey presto!

Stuffed Mushrooms

1 tablespoon extra virgin olive oil, plus extra for greasing

9 oz/250 g (about 12) closed cup mushrooms, cremini or white, stems removed and set aside

2 shallots, peeled and finely chopped

1 garlic clove, peeled and chopped

1 teaspoon finely chopped rosemary

3 slices of Serrano ham or prosciutto, finely sliced

2 oz/50 g goat's cheese

4 tablespoons fresh breadcrumbs

salt and freshly ground black pepper

Serves 4–6 as part of a selection of tapas

Preheat the oven to 375°F/190°C. Lightly grease a baking sheet. Wipe the mushrooms with a damp paper towel to remove any dirt. Roughly chop the mushroom stems and set aside.

Heat the olive oil in a large, nonstick skillet and sauté the shallots for 2–3 minutes, or until soft and translucent but not browned. Add the garlic, rosemary, mushroom stems, and black pepper to taste and sauté for a couple of minutes. Add the ham and stir to combine.

Remove from the heat and transfer to a bowl. Stir in the goat's cheese and breadcrumbs and season to taste. Place 1 heaped teaspoon of the mixture into each mushroom and place on the baking sheet.

Bake for 8–10 minutes, or until lightly golden and the mushrooms are cooked. Serve hot.

Nothing is more thirst-quenching on a hot summer's afternoon than a small cup of gazpacho on ice; alternatively, you can heat it up for a winter warmer. Gazpacho was originally made by field workers, who combined their oil and bread rations with water and salt and added whatever vegetables they had available—namely tomatoes and peppers—to produce a thick vegetable soup.

Gazpacho

about 2½ oz/60 g
stale white bread
(about 2–3 slices)

1 small red onion,
peeled and chopped

½ cucumber
(7 oz/200 g)
peeled, seeded and
cut into pieces

1½ lb/675 g (about
8 medium) tomatoes,
skinned and seeded

1 red bell pepper,
seeded and chopped

2 garlic cloves, peeled
and finely chopped

1 teaspoon toasted
cumin seeds

½–1 teaspoon
Spanish hot smoked
paprika, to taste

1 tablespoon extra
virgin olive oil

2 tablespoons sherry
vinegar or red
wine vinegar

a pinch of sugar
(optional, depending
on the sweetness of
your tomatoes)

3½ tablespoons
ice-cold water

salt and freshly
ground black pepper

Serves 6

Put the bread in a shallow dish, cover with water and leave to soak for 10–15 minutes, but no longer. Squeeze the water from the bread with your hands.

Put the onion in a separate bowl, cover with boiling water and leave to soak for the same time. Drain the onion.

Put the bread, onion, cucumber, tomatoes, chopped pepper, garlic, cumin seeds, paprika, and olive oil in a food processor. Whiz well, then add the vinegar, sugar, if needed, and the water. Push the soup through a fine strainer, adding a little extra chilled water if it is too thick. Season to taste, cover and chill until needed.

To serve, pour into small glasses or bowls, over ice if liked.

Not typically Spanish, but these little tartlets show the benefit of seasonal cooking. For more rustic and hearty tartlets, choose a selection of wild mushrooms in the fall.

Mixed Mushroom and Eggplant Tartlets

1 large eggplant

1½ tablespoons extra virgin olive oil

13 oz/375 g puff pastry

2 oz/50 g soft goat's cheese

11 oz/300 g mixed mushrooms, such as porcini, chanterelles, button, chopped into small chunks or slices

a good splosh (about 2 tbsp) of any type of Madeira or sherry

a small handful of fresh flat-leaf parsley, chopped

salt and freshly ground black pepper

Makes 12–16

Preheat the oven to 400°F/200°C. Put the eggplant on a baking sheet, brush with about 1 teaspoon of the olive oil and bake for 25–30 minutes, or until soft and cooked. Remove from the oven and leave to cool slightly.

While the eggplant is cooling, cut the puff pastry into 12–16 rounds about 3 inches/7 cm in diameter. Place on a baking sheet and impress a second round into each, about 2½ inches/6 cm in diameter, ensuring that you do not cut right through. Bake in the oven for 8–12 minutes, or until golden and puffed.

When they are cooked, remove from the oven and, using a small knife, cut around the inner circle and remove the disk of pastry. This can be used as a top if liked, or pushed down into the case.

Now, peel the eggplant and mix with the goat's cheese, then season to taste and set aside.

Heat the remaining olive oil in a large skillet and sauté the mushrooms until golden brown. While the pan is still hot, add the Madeira or sherry and let it evaporate. Stir through the parsley and season well.

Put a spoonful of eggplant mixture and a heaped pile of mushrooms into each pastry case and serve warm or cool.

If you are on a wheat-free diet, these tarts are a treat. The heart of the artichoke is scooped out and shaped into a "tart" case, which is then filled with this delicious pancetta mixture. They can easily be made into a vegetarian's dream, too, by leaving out the pancetta.

Artichoke, Pea, and Pancetta Tarts

6 large globe artichoke

juice of 1 lemon

1 cup/250 ml white wine

1 cup/250 ml passata (crushed tomatoes)

2 sprigs fresh rosemary

2 tablespoons extra virgin olive oil

¾ cup/100 g peas, fresh or frozen

2 shallots or baby onions, peeled and finely chopped

5 oz/150 g cubed pancetta

1 egg, beaten

1 tablespoon milk

3 oz/75 g goat's cheese

Makes 6

Firstly, prepare the artichokes. Using a sharp knife, slice each stem off at the base and snap away the leaves one by one and discard them. Trim the base of any dark green bits and use a small spoon to dig out the furry choke. Rub the artichokes immediately with lemon juice and put the bases into a small saucepan.

Add the wine, passata, 1 rosemary sprig, and 1 tablespoon of olive oil to the pan. Bring to a boil, then reduce the heat and simmer for 20–25 minutes, or until the bases are tender. Leave to cool in the liquid.

When you are ready to cook them, preheat the oven to 400°F/200°C. Bring a small saucepan of water to a boil and blanch the peas for 2–3 minutes, or until just cooked. Cool them under running cold water and set aside.

Heat the remaining oil in a large, nonstick skillet. Finely chop the remaining rosemary sprig, then add to the pan with the chopped onion and pancetta and sauté until golden. Remove from the heat and stir in the peas.

To assemble the tartlets, remove the artichoke bases from the liquid and pat dry. Place them flat on a baking sheet and spoon the pancetta mixture into them. Combine the beaten egg and milk and spoon over the tartlets, then crumble over the goat's cheese.

Bake in the oven for 10–15 minutes, or until the filling is set and lightly golden.

Serve warm or cold, either whole or cut into quarters.

A springtime treat that is delicious served with a platter of cold cuts.
Try adding some fresh peas, lima beans, or broad beans to the omelet
for an extra dose of greens.

Asparagus Omelet

9 oz/250 g asparagus, trimmed

1 tablespoon extra virgin olive oil

1 onion, peeled and finely chopped

1 garlic clove, peeled and crushed

½ cup/50 g finely grated Parmesan or Manchego cheese

6 large eggs, beaten

salt and freshly ground black pepper

Makes 12 tapas-sized portions

Cut the asparagus into 1 inch/2.5 cm pieces and blanch in boiling water for 3–4 minutes, then drain. Run the pieces under cold water until cool, then set aside.

Heat the olive oil to medium in a 12 inch/30 cm nonstick skillet. Sauté the onion for 2–3 minutes, or until softened and cooked but not browned. Add the garlic and asparagus and sauté for a further minute, then stir in the cheese and season generously with salt and black pepper. Pour in the beaten eggs and shake the pan so that everything is evenly distributed, but do not stir. Reduce the heat, cover the pan and leave to cook for 8–10 minutes, or until the egg is set.

Remove from the heat and serve warm or cold, cut into small wedges or squares.

This recipe uses mealy potatoes, which have a low moisture content and are higher in starch than waxy potatoes. They may start to disintegrate slightly while you're frying them, but this just adds to the texture of the tortilla. In some parts of Spain they make their tortilla completely with mashed potato, so this is somewhat of a compromise.

Spanish Tortilla (Tortilla Española)

5 tablespoons extra virgin olive oil

about 6 medium (2¼ lb/1 kg) mealy potatoes, such as Russet, peeled, quartered and thinly sliced (⅛ inch/ 2–3 mm thick)

1 medium onion, peeled and thinly sliced

6 large eggs

salt

Makes 12 tapas-sized portions

Heat the olive oil in a 10–12 inch/25–30 cm nonstick skillet. Sauté the sliced potatoes and onion, lifting and turning them until cooked but not brown—this will take 15–20 minutes.

Beat the eggs together in a large mixing bowl and season well with salt. When the potatoes are cooked, using a slotted spoon, transfer them into the egg mixture, leaving as much oil behind as possible. Strain the oil from the pan and reserve.

Heat 1 tablespoon of the reserved oil in the same pan over a medium heat. Add the egg and potato mixture, spreading the potatoes evenly in the pan. Cook the tortilla, covered, for 5–6 minutes, gently shaking the pan so that it doesn't stick.

Slide a long spatula underneath the tortilla, then place a large plate over it and quickly turn it over on to the plate. Add another tablespoon of oil to the pan and quickly slide the tortilla back in. Tuck the sides in with a fork and cook for a further 3–4 minutes, or until it is firm and set.

Remove the tortilla from the pan and leave to cool to room temperature before serving, cut into wedges.

Grated carrots don't always need to remind you of your childhood. Try this salad, which with the addition of haloumi and harissa is a grown-up's dream!

Carrot, Haloumi, and Harissa Salad

1 lb 2 oz/500 g (about 3 large) carrots, peeled

1 small bunch of fresh flat-leaf parsley, roughly chopped

2 tablespoons extra virgin olive oil

9 oz/250 g haloumi cheese, cut into ½ inch/1 cm cubes

For the marinade

4 tablespoons extra virgin olive oil

1 teaspoon caraway seeds

1 teaspoon cumin seeds

1 garlic clove, peeled and crushed

2 teaspoons harissa paste

2 tablespoons red wine vinegar

1 teaspoon superfine sugar

Serves 4–6 as part of a selection of tapas

Grate the carrots into a large bowl, then set aside while you prepare the marinade.

Heat the olive oil in a small saucepan or skillet and add the caraway and cumin seeds, the garlic, and harissa paste. Cook for 1–2 minutes, or until aromatic and the garlic turns golden in color. Remove from the heat and stir in the vinegar and sugar. Pour over the carrots, mix well and set aside in the refrigerator to marinate for at least 1 hour, or up to 24 hours.

Just before serving, remove the carrot from the refrigerator to bring it back to room temperature and stir in the parsley. Heat the olive oil in a skillet to medium hot, then add the haloumi cubes and fry for 3–5 minutes, or until golden brown. Remove from the heat and drain on paper towels. Allow to cool slightly, then mix into the carrot.

You'll find this dish throughout Spain in many different shapes and forms. Really, it's just fried potatoes in a spicy tomato sauce. Sometimes peppers might be added to the sauce, or the potatoes may be thinly sliced and fried rather than cut into chunks.

114 Spicy Fried Potatoes (Patatas Bravas)

4 tablespoons extra virgin olive oil

6 medium (about 2¼ lb/1 kg) mealy potatoes, such as Russet, peeled and cut into 1¾ inch/ 4 cm cubes

1 large onion, peeled and finely chopped

2 garlic cloves, peeled and finely chopped

2 red chiles, seeded and finely chopped, or ½–1 teaspoon dried crushed chiles

½ teaspoon ground cumin

2 tablespoons red wine vinegar

14 oz/400 ml can chopped tomatoes

1 teaspoon superfine sugar

salt

Serves 4–6 as part of a selection of tapas

Preheat the oven to 425°F/220°C. Heat 3 tablespoons of the olive oil in a large, nonstick skillet until hot. Add the potatoes and sauté until golden brown all over. Transfer the potatoes and any remaining oil to a baking dish and cook in the oven until the potatoes are crisp—about 15 minutes.

While the potatoes are cooking, prepare the sauce. Heat the remaining olive oil in a skillet over medium heat. Sauté the onion for 2–3 minutes, or until cooked and translucent but not browned.

Add the garlic, chiles, and cumin and sauté for a further 2 minutes. Add the remaining ingredients and simmer the sauce for a further 10–12 minutes.

Drain the potatoes from the oil (if there is any remaining) and place in one large or several small serving dishes. Pour over the sauce and serve hot.

Waxy potatoes have a high moisture content and are low in starch. They will tend to hold their shape a lot better than mealy potatoes and are ideal in salads, or in recipes such as this where potatoes are boiled or roasted.

The red paprika oils will leech out from the sausages, giving this salad a fiery tinge. I like to use "picante," or "hot," sausages, but it's up to you.

Saffron Potatoes, Egg, and Watercress

Chickpea and Chorizo Salad

6 medium (about 1 kg/2¼ lb) waxy potatoes, such as Yukon gold

4 tablespoons extra virgin olive oil

½ stick/50 g butter

a large pinch of saffron threads

4–6 eggs, boiled for 5 minutes, then plunged into cold water and peeled

1 bunch of watercress, washed and trimmed to remove any coarse stalks

Alioli (see page 19), to serve (optional)

sea salt and freshly ground pepper

Serves 4–6 as part of a selection of tapas

Boil the potatoes in their skins until cooked but still firm—10–12 minutes. Allow to cool slightly, then peel and cut each into 8–10 wedges.

Heat the olive oil and butter in a large, nonstick skillet until the butter starts to foam. Add the saffron and potatoes and cook until the potatoes are tender and golden in color. Season generously with salt and black pepper, then put the potatoes on one large or several small plates.

Cut the eggs in half lengthwise and place on top of the potatoes, yolk-side up. Scatter over the watercress and serve with a generous dollop of alioli.

½ tablespoon extra virgin olive oil

2 (about 7 oz/200 g) cooking chorizo sausages, sliced lengthwise then into 1 cm/½ inch pieces

1 red bell pepper, seeded and diced into ½ inch/1 cm cubes

2 tablespoons dry Madeira, or red wine

14 oz/400 g can chickpeas, drained and rinsed

3 scallions, trimmed and finely sliced

fine salt and freshly ground black pepper

Serves 4–6 as part of a selection of tapas

Heat the olive oil in a large, nonstick skillet and cook the chorizo and diced bell pepper for 3–4 minutes.

Add the Madeira and sauté for a further 30 seconds, then add the chickpeas and cook until the chickpeas are hot and the chorizo is thoroughly cooked.

Remove from the heat and stir in the scallions and seasoning to taste. Serve warm with crusty bread.

This is basically a Catalan version of roasted vegetables.
Slow-cooked and delicious, they are also a perfect accompaniment
to meat or fish dishes.

Escalivada

2 red bell peppers

1 medium eggplant

2 small red onions

4 tomatoes

**3 garlic cloves,
unpeeled**

**3–4 tablespoons extra
virgin olive oil**

juice of 1 lemon

**salt and freshly
ground black pepper**

*Serves 4–6 as part of
a selection of tapas*

Preheat the oven to 400°F/200°C. Wash all the vegetables well and dry
them using paper towels. Lay them in a single layer with the garlic on
a large baking sheet and add just enough olive oil to lightly coat them—
2–3 tablespoons. Season with salt and black pepper.

Roast in the oven for 20–25 minutes, or until they are soft but still
holding their shape and the skins are loosened and slightly charred in
parts. Remove from the oven and leave to cool.

When the vegetables are cool, peel off all the skins and chop the
vegetables into large chunks. Squeeze the garlic from their skins.
Arrange on a platter, or in small tapas dishes.

Combine the lemon juice and remaining olive oil in a separate bowl and
season well. Pour over the vegetables and serve warm or cold.

These deep-fried rice croquettes are more popular in the north than in the south of Spain. There they use the short-grained paella rice that is prolific in the plains of Catalonia. These rice balls must be eaten warm so that the cheesy Manchego center oozes as you bite into it.

Spanish Rice Balls with Melting Manchego Centers

1 tablespoon extra virgin olive oil

1 tablespoon butter

1 onion, peeled and finely diced

a pinch of saffron threads

a pinch of turmeric

1 garlic clove, peeled and crushed

1¾ cups/300 g Spanish paella rice

3 cups/750 ml hot vegetable stock

1 heaping cup/150 g frozen or fresh peas

4 cups/1 liter sunflower or vegetable oil

2 eggs, lightly beaten

3½ oz/100 g Manchego cheese, cut into 1 cm/ ½ inch cubes

1 cup/100 g dried breadcrumbs

salt and freshly ground black pepper

Makes 36–40

Heat the olive oil and butter in a large, nonstick skillet. Add the onion and sauté for 2–3 minutes, or until translucent but not browned. Stir in the saffron, turmeric, and garlic and sauté for a further minute. Add the rice and stir through until slightly translucent around the edges.

Pour in all the hot stock and bring to a boil. Reduce the heat to a simmer and leave to simmer for 20–25 minutes, adding the peas after 15 minutes and stirring occasionally, or until the rice is cooked and the liquid is absorbed. Season well, tasting as you do so, and set aside to cool completely.

Pour the sunflower or vegetable oil into a large, heavy-bottomed saucepan and put over a low heat while you prepare the rice balls.

Add the beaten eggs to the cooled rice mixture and stir well to combine. Take golf ball-sized amounts of the mixture and shape into rounds. Press a piece of cheese into the center of each round and shape the ball around it. Roll each ball in breadcrumbs and set aside on a lightly crumbed board.

The oil is hot enough when a small cube of bread dropped into it turns golden in about 30 seconds. Place 4–5 balls into the oil at a time and cook for 3–4 minutes, or until they are evenly golden. Remove each batch with a slotted spoon and drain on paper towels while you cook the rest. They can be kept warm in a low oven as you go.

Serve warm so that the cheese center oozes out.

If you're having trouble with your pan and the tortilla seems to be sticking—don't panic! Don't attempt to flip it, but instead heat up the broiler and finish cooking the top of the tortilla under the broiler.

Once the tortilla is cooked and cooled slightly, use a long spatula to loosen the bottom and you should be able to flip the tortilla straight out on to a plate.

120 Red and Green Bell Pepper Tortilla

⅔ cup/150 ml extra virgin olive oil

about 4 medium (1 lb 5½ oz/600 g) mealy potatoes, such as Russet, peeled, quartered and thinly sliced (⅛ inch/ 2–3 mm thick)

1 medium onion, peeled and thinly sliced

1 red bell pepper, seeded and thinly sliced

1 green bell pepper, seeded and thinly sliced

6 large eggs

salt

Makes 12 tapas-sized portions

Heat the olive oil in a 10–12 inch/25–30 cm nonstick skillet. Sauté the sliced potatoes, onion, and peppers, lifting and turning them until cooked but not brown—this will take 15–20 minutes.

Beat the eggs together in a large mixing bowl and season well with salt. When the potatoes are cooked, using a slotted spoon, transfer them into the egg mixture, leaving as much oil behind as possible. Strain the oil from the pan and reserve.

Heat 1 tablespoon of the reserved oil in the same pan over medium heat. Add the egg and potato mixture, spreading the potatoes evenly in the pan. Cook the tortilla, uncovered, for 5–6 minutes, gently shaking the pan so that it doesn't stick.

Slide a long spatula underneath the tortilla, then place a large plate over it and quickly turn it over on to the plate. Add another tablespoon of oil to the pan and quickly slide the tortilla back in. Tuck the sides in with a fork and cook for a further 3–4 minutes, or until firm and set.

Remove the tortilla from the pan and leave to cool to room temperature before serving, cut into wedges.

I prefer these served as a cold dish, since the flavor seems to develop more and more. If you're trying to impress, keep the little green ends on the carrots and add a touch of honey for sweetness.

You don't need to stick strictly to the vegetables listed below—for a change, try using cauliflower, pumpkin, or asparagus. If you don't want to make up any of the suggested accompaniments below, a bought sweet chili sauce also goes well, or a squeeze of lime juice.

Paprika and Cumin-Spiced Carrots

11 oz/300 g baby carrots, trimmed (see above)

1 teaspoon cumin seeds

1 tablespoon sesame seeds

1 teaspoon ground coriander

1 teaspoon Spanish hot smoked paprika

½ teaspoon fine salt

1 teaspoon superfine sugar

2 tablespoons extra virgin olive oil

1 tablespoon red wine vinegar

1 small bunch of fresh flat-leaf parsley, finely chopped

Cook the carrots in boiling water for 3–4 minutes, or until cooked but still firm to the bite, or al dente. Rinse them under cold running water and set aside.

Toast the cumin and sesame seeds in a dry, heavy-bottomed saucepan until fragrant and golden. Remove from the heat and stir in the ground coriander, paprika, salt, sugar, olive oil, vinegar, and parsley.

Stir this mixture into the warm carrots and serve immediately, or set aside to cool.

Serves 4–6 as part of a selection of tapas

Battered Vegetables

1¼ cups/150 g all-purpose flour, plus extra for coating

2 oz/50 g cornstarch

1 cup/250 ml cold water

a pinch of salt

½ teaspoon white wine vinegar

1 large egg yolk

1 large zucchini, thinly sliced on the diagonal

1 eggplant, thinly sliced crossways

1 red bell pepper, seeded and cut lengthwise into ¾ inch/ 1.5 cm wide strips

1 onion, peeled and thickly sliced

3–4 cups/750 ml– 1 liter vegetable or sunflower oil

Sweet Chile and Red Bell Pepper Salsa or Alioli, to serve (see pages 29, 19)

Put the flour and cornstarch in a large mixing bowl. Slowly whisk in the water to form a smooth paste. Add the salt, vinegar, and egg yolk and mix well. Refrigerate the batter for at least 15 minutes, or up to 1 hour.

Prepare the vegetables and set aside. Heat the oil in a heavy-bottomed saucepan to 375ºF/190ºC, or until a small cube of bread turns golden in about 30 seconds. Dip the vegetables in flour, then in the batter and deep-fry in batches for 3–4 minutes, or until golden and cooked.

Remove with a slotted spoon and drain on paper towels. Serve immediately with Sweet Chile and Red Bell Pepper Salsa or Alioli for dipping.

Serves 4–6 as part of a selection of tapas

The color, flavor and aroma of honey depend on the flower that the nectar has been taken from. Orange blossom honey brings the Spanish element to this dish, but choose whatever flavor you like best, from the subtle to the more fragrant.

Fried Goat's Cheese Balls with Honey

⅔ cup/75 g all-purpose flour

1 egg, lightly beaten

1 cup/75 g breadcrumbs

12 balls (about 7 oz/200 g) goat's cheese, drained, or a 7 oz/200 g chunk, cut into 1 inch/ 2.5 cm cubes

3 cups/750 ml vegetable or sunflower oil

2–3 tablespoons honey

Makes about 12

Put the flour, egg, and breadcrumbs in three separate bowls and line them up in order. Dust the goat's cheese balls in the flour, dip them in the beaten egg, then roll them in the breadcrumbs. Set aside and refrigerate until you are ready to cook.

Heat the vegetable or sunflower oil in a large, heavy-bottomed saucepan to 375°F/190°C, or until a small cube of bread turns golden in about 30 seconds. Cook the balls for 3–4 minutes, or until golden brown and the cheese is oozing in the center. Remove with a slotted spoon and drain on paper towels.

Transfer to a serving plate, drizzle over the honey and serve immediately with cocktail sticks or wooden toothpicks.

This salad is refreshing on the palate and cleansing to the liver.
For a more dramatic look, use blood oranges when they're in season.
I sometimes like to add a tin of white tuna in oil for a slightly more
substantial tapa.

124   Valencia Orange, Fennel, and Black Olive Salad

**3 Valencia oranges,
or other juicy oranges
such as blood or navel**

1 fennel bulb

**¾ cup/75–100 g
black olives**

**3 tablespoons extra
virgin olive oil**

juice of 1 lemon

**freshly ground
black pepper**

**a small handful of
fresh flat-leaf parsley,
finely chopped,
to serve**

*Serves 4–6 as part of
a selection of tapas*

Peel the oranges, removing all the white pith, then finely slice. Using a mandoline or very sharp knife, finely shave the fennel into thin slices. Combine the oranges, fennel, and olives in a large bowl.

In a separate bowl, combine the olive oil, lemon juice, and black pepper. Pour this dressing over the salad, gently combine and leave to marinate in the refrigerator for at least 1 hour, or up to 12 hours.

Just before serving, scatter over the parsley leaves and serve cold.

If you're serving them hard-cooked, regular eggs would work just as well in this recipe. Use 4–6 and, once cooked, cut them into quarters lengthwise.

Quail Eggs with Paprika Sesame Salt

127

24 quail eggs

For the spice mix

1 tablespoon coriander seeds

1 tablespoon cumin seeds

2 tablespoons white sesame seeds

2 tablespoons sea salt flakes

1 teaspoon freshly ground black pepper

½ teaspoon Spanish hot smoked paprika

Makes 24

Put the quail eggs in a pan and cover with cold water. Bring to a boil and cook for 2½ minutes for soft-cooked, or 3½ minutes for hard-cooked. Drain the eggs and cool them under running cold water. Reserve a few eggs in their shells for garnish and peel the remainder, then set aside.

Heat a heavy-bottomed skillet to medium heat and add the coriander, cumin, and sesame seeds and the salt. Stir continuously for 2–3 minutes, or until the seeds are aromatic and slightly golden. Transfer to a mortar and, using a pestle, roughly crush the seeds but do not grind to a fine powder. Stir in the black pepper and paprika, then put the spice mix in a small dish.

Put the peeled eggs in a bowl, garnish with the whole eggs and serve with the spice mix for dipping.

Sherry is a wine full of intense depth and complex flavors. Produced in Jerez, in southern Spain, it has a rich history and has always been an essential part of Spanish cuisine. It comes in many different styles, from pale golden and dry to the dark and rich with a soft sweet finish.

This goat's cheese and pepper combo is a match made in heaven. The sweet, succulent peppers can be topped with a small cube of quince paste, but it's optional. If you are stuck for time, just buy a jar of piquillo peppers (see page 102) and use them in the same way.

Mushrooms with Garlic and Sherry

3 tablespoons extra virgin olive oil

½ stick/50 g butter

4–6 garlic cloves, peeled and sliced

a pinch of Spanish hot smoked paprika

1 lb 2 oz/500 g button mushrooms, sliced into ¼ inch/5 mm thick slices

salt

3 tablespoons dry or sweet sherry

1 tablespoon fresh flat-leaf parsley, roughly chopped

Serves 4–6 as part of a selection of tapas

Heat the olive oil and butter in a large, nonstick skillet to medium hot. Add the garlic and paprika and sauté briefly but do not brown.

Increase the heat and add the mushrooms, then sauté, stirring constantly, until golden and the oil has been absorbed. Season with salt. Add the sherry and simmer briefly so that the flavor can be absorbed.

Remove from the heat, sprinkle over the parsley and serve immediately.

Trio of Roasted Peppers with Goat's Cheese

3 bell peppers, preferably 1 each of red, yellow and orange, or a mix

1 tablespoon extra virgin olive oil, plus extra to serve

1 tablespoon honey

2 large sprigs fresh thyme

3½ oz/100 g goat's cheese, cut into 12 chunks

3–3½ oz/75–100 g Quince Paste (Membrillo, see page 30), cut into small cubes (optional)

sea salt and freshly ground black pepper

Makes 12 tapas-sized portions

Preheat the oven to 350°F/180°C. Cut each pepper in half, seed and remove the core, then halve again. Place the peppers, cut-side up, in a single layer on a baking sheet. Drizzle the olive oil and honey over the peppers, then roughly tear over the thyme sprigs and season generously with salt and black pepper.

Roast in the oven for 18–20 minutes, or until cooked and slightly charred around the edges. Remove from the oven and leave to cool for 20–30 minutes.

When the peppers are cool enough to handle, place a cube of goat's cheese and quince paste, if using, in the center of each. Roll up and secure with a cocktail stick or wooden toothpick. Serve warm, drizzled with some olive oil.

Roasting asparagus really intensifies its flavor. Sprinkled with sea salt and some of your finest extra virgin olive oil, the stems are perfect as they are, but sometimes we want something just a little bit more special and that's why I've included my recipe for tarragon salsa verde.

White asparagus is cut while it is below the ground—the lack of light prevents the production of chlorophyll and the asparagus from turning green. Fresh white asparagus must be peeled up to the tip to remove the tough outer skin, and needs longer cooking than green asparagus.

Roasted Asparagus with Salsa Verde

White Asparagus with Dipping Sauces

1 lb 2 oz/500 g asparagus, trimmed

1 tablespoon extra virgin olive oil

sea salt and freshly ground black pepper

For the salsa verde

1 small red onion, peeled and very finely diced

1 garlic clove, peeled and crushed

2 canned anchovies in oil, drained and finely chopped

1 tablespoon capers, roughly chopped

½ teaspoon Dijon mustard

1 tablespoon cider vinegar

1 tablespoon finely chopped tarragon

1 tablespoon finely chopped fresh flat-leaf parsley

about 4 tablespoons extra virgin olive oil

Serves 4–6 as part of a selection of tapas

Preheat the oven to 350°F/180°C. Place the asparagus in a single layer on a baking pan with shallow sides. Sprinkle generously with salt and pepper and drizzle over the olive oil. Roast in the oven for 10–12 minutes (depending on the thickness of the asparagus), or until tender to the bite and cooked through.

While the asparagus are cooking, combine all the ingredients for the salsa verde in a bowl and mix well, adding extra olive oil if liked. Season to taste.

Serve the asparagus warm with the salsa verde drizzled over, or as a dipping sauce.

1 bunch of fresh white asparagus, or 12 oz/350 g jar (about 8–12 stems) white asparagus

1 tablespoon extra virgin olive oil

½ cup/100 ml Alioli (see page 19)

1 tablespoon chopped fresh dill

½ cup/100 ml Romesco Sauce (see page 15)

Serves 4–6 as part of a selection of tapas

If using fresh asparagus, peel the stems and drop them into cold water.

Heat 1 tablespoon olive oil in a skillet. Add the asparagus and turn to coat them in the oil, stirring continuously so that they don't color, then add about 1 cup/250 ml of water. Cover and leave to simmer for 3–4 minutes, then remove the lid and simmer until the water has evaporated and the asparagus are cooked. If using cooked asparagus in a jar, drain and place on a serving platter.

Combine the alioli and dill in a small bowl and mix well. Put the herbed alioli and the romesco sauce in two separate serving bowls and place on the same platter as the asparagus. To eat, dip the asparagus in the sauces.

These small pies are popular in Spain. This vegetarian version is baked, rather than deep-fried, as is normal. The rich buttery pastry wrapped around salty olives and cheese melts-in-your-mouth when served warm. These are delicious served with an ice-cold glass of fino sherry.

Cheese and Olive Empanadas

1 quantity Empanada Pastry (see page 31), or 1 lb 2 oz/500 g bought puff pastry

200 g/7 oz soft goat's or sheep's cheese

1 egg, lightly beaten

¾ cup/100 g pitted green olives, roughly chopped

all-purpose flour, for dusting

¼ stick/30 g butter, melted

freshly ground black pepper

Makes 24–30

Prepare the pastry and refrigerate until ready to assemble the pies. Preheat the oven to 400°F/200°C.

Put the cheese, egg, and chopped olives in a bowl and mix well, then season with black pepper.

Roll the pastry out on a lightly floured surface to approximately ⅛–¼ inch/3–5 mm thick and, using a 3½–4 inch/9–10 cm round cutter, cut out circles.

Place a heaped teaspoon of the filling on one half of each round of pastry. Dip your finger in water and slightly dampen the pastry edges (to help them stick), then fold the pastry over the filling to make a half-moon shape. To seal the empanadas, pinch the edges of the pastry firmly together, then press down on the edges with the prongs of a fork to finish.

Brush the empanadas with melted butter and bake in the oven for 15–18 minutes, or until golden and puffed. Serve hot or warm.

Manchego is a sheep's cheese and varies from mild and quite soft to strong and hard. I like to choose the more mature and intensely flavored variety for this tapas dish. The cheese melts and becomes oozy, so they must be eaten quickly while still hot.

Deep-Fried Manchego Cubes with Membrillo

3½ oz/100 g
all-purpose flour

1 egg, lightly beaten

1 cup/100 g dried
breadcrumbs

7 oz/200 g Manchego
cheese, cut into
1 inch/2.5 cm cubes

3–4 cups/750 ml–
1 liter vegetable or
sunflower oil

3½ oz/100 g Quince
Paste (Membrillo, see
page 30), cut into
½ inch/1 cm cubes

Put the flour, egg, and breadcrumbs in three separate bowls and line them up in order. Coat the cheese cubes heavily in the flour, dip them in the beaten egg, then roll them in the breadcrumbs. Set aside on a lightly floured board.

Heat the vegetable or sunflower oil in a large saucepan to 375°F/190°C, or until a small cube of bread turns golden in about 30 seconds. Cook the cheese cubes for 1–2 minutes, or until golden brown—the cheese inside should be soft and melted. Remove with a slotted spoon and drain on paper towels.

Place a cube of membrillo on top of each cheese cube and secure with a cocktail stick or wooden toothpick. Transfer to a serving plate and serve immediately while still warm and oozy.

Makes 20

Serve the following as part of a selection of tapas: throw them together into a salad and drizzle with extra virgin olive oil, or serve alongside toasted breads or crostini as toppings.

Roasted Garlic

1 large, unpeeled garlic bulb

extra virgin olive oil

Preheat the oven to 300°F/150°C. Rub the whole garlic bulb lightly with oil, place in a roasting dish and cover the dish with foil.

Roast in the oven for 1–1½ hours depending on the size of the garlic, until it is very soft and tender. (Older garlic may take longer, so don't rush it.)

Allow to cool, then squeeze the flesh out of each clove.

Roasted Bell Peppers

a selection of bell peppers—red, yellow, orange and green, washed and dried

Preheat the oven to 400°F/200°C. Place the bell peppers on a large roasting pan and roast for 25–30 minutes, or until softened and slightly charred.

Allow to cool completely, then cut each in half, seed and peel.

Roasted Eggplants

1 large eggplant

extra virgin olive oil

Preheat the oven to 400°F/200°C. Lightly rub the eggplant with a little olive oil and place on a baking sheet. Roast in the oven for 25–30 minutes, or until soft and slightly charred.

Allow to cool completely, then peel.

Roasted Cherry Tomatoes

2–3 bunches cherry tomatoes on the vine

1–1½ tablespoons extra virgin olive oil, plus extra to serve

sea salt and freshly ground black pepper

Preheat the oven to 400°F/200°C. Put the tomatoes on a baking sheet and drizzle over the olive oil. Season generously, then roast for 15–20 minutes, or until cooked and the juices are starting to ooze.

Serve warm or cold as a garnish, or on their own, drizzled with some of the finest extra virgin olive oil.

Haloumi is both salty in taste and squeaky in texture, with a firmness that holds its shape when cooked. It has an almost meaty substance, so it can be a good alternative for vegetarians. Dress it like you would a salad, and serve with a few salad leaves on the side—delicious.

136 Grilled Haloumi with Herbs

11 oz/300 g haloumi cheese, cut into 8–10 slices about ½ inch/1 cm thick

1½ tablespoons extra virgin olive oil, plus extra to serve

For the dressing

4 tablespoons extra virgin olive oil

juice and zest of 1 lemon

½ teaspoon Spanish sweet smoked paprika

2 tablespoons chopped fresh herbs, such as parsley, cilantro, chives, mint

freshly ground black pepper

Serves 4 as part of a selection of tapas

Preheat a griddle pan to very hot. Rub the haloumi slices lightly with olive oil and grill them for 2–3 minutes on each side, or until grill marks form and the cheese is warmed through.

Combine all the dressing ingredients in a small bowl. Pour some dressing over the hot haloumi and serve immediately, or leave to cool. You can serve the extra dressing on the side for people to add to taste.

This hearty gratin is best made in small tapas dishes and served with several forks so that everyone can dig in. They can be prepared in advance up to the last stage. Just bake them off, or reheat them in the oven when needed so that they are steaming hot and golden brown.

Eggplant, Manchego, and Piquillo Pepper Gratin

2 large eggplants, about 1½ lb/675 g total weight

olive oil, for brushing

¼ stick/30 g butter

2 tablespoons all-purpose flour

2½ cups/600 ml cold milk

1 cup/75 g finely grated Manchego cheese

1 egg, lightly beaten

9 oz/250 g piquillo peppers (see page 102)

salt and freshly ground black pepper

Makes 6 small or 1 large tapas

Preheat the broiler to very hot and preheat the oven to 400°F/200°C. Cut the eggplants into ½ inch/1 cm thick slices and brush with olive oil. Chargrill the eggplants for 2–3 minutes on one side and about 2 minutes on the other side, or until cooked and soft. Set aside while you make the sauce.

Melt the butter in a heavy-bottomed saucepan. Stir in the flour and cook, stirring, until it turns yellow—this means the roux is cooked. Stir in the milk, little by little to avoid lumps, and continue beating until the mixture thickens. It should be thick enough to coat the back of a spoon. Remove from the heat and stir in two-thirds of the cheese. Season to taste and leave to cool slightly, then stir in the beaten egg.

Use six individual tapas plates or ramekins, or one larger ovenproof dish. Layer the eggplant, sauce, and peppers alternately into the plates, ramekins, or dish, finishing with the peppers. Sprinkle over the remaining cheese and a good grind of black pepper. Bake in the oven for 15–20 minutes, or until bubbling and golden. Serve hot or warm.

Manchego (sheep's cheese) and membrillo (quince paste) is an inspired union of flavors. Produced in the region of La Mancha, Manchego is one of Spain's iconic symbols and can now be found in many supermarkets worldwide.

Manchego with Membrillo (Quince Paste)

3½ oz/100 g wedge Manchego cheese, at room temperature

3½ oz/100 g Quince Paste (Membrillo, see page 30), or bought membrillo

Makes 6 tapas-sized portions

Trim the rind from the cheese and cut into six wedges. Place the cheese in a single layer on individual plates, or on one large plate.

Slice the quince paste into six pieces and place one slice on top of each wedge of cheese. Serve.

After sampling this tapa in a bar in the heart of Valencia, my friend
Sara and I thought it impossible to bring this salad to life. The key is to
not overcook the vegetables, use fresh not frozen, and don't drown it
in mayo. Probably not traditional at all now, but much more tasty!

Russian Salad

3½ oz/100 g
new potatoes

½ cup/50 g freshly
shelled peas

3½ oz/100 g good
quality white canned
tuna in olive oil

1 hard-cooked egg,
roughly chopped

2 tablespoons
mayonnaise

1 tablespoon snipped
fresh chives, plus
extra to garnish

a pinch of Spanish
sweet smoked paprika

1 Belgian endive,
separated into leaves

salt and freshly
ground black pepper

*Serves 4–6 as part of
a selection of tapas*

Boil the potatoes for 8–10 minutes, or until cooked but still firm.
Run them under cold water and leave to cool, then cut into cubes
about ½ inch/1 cm.

Cook the peas in boiling water for 2–3 minutes, or until just cooked.
Cool completely under running cold water.

Combine all the ingredients, except the Belgian endive, in a bowl and
season to taste. Set aside until you are ready to serve.

Separate the Belgian endive into individual leaves, wash and carefully
dry, using paper towels. Place the leaves on a plate, cup-side up.
Spoon the salad mixture into the leaves and serve garnished with
extra chives.

Index

143